Antiquities of the Mesa Verde National Park

Spruce-tree House

Jesse Walter Fewkes

Alpha Editions

This edition published in 2024

ISBN : 9789367245231

Design and Setting By
Alpha Editions
www.alphaedis.com
Email - info@alphaedis.com

As per information held with us this book is in Public Domain.
This book is a reproduction of an important historical work. Alpha Editions uses the best technology to reproduce historical work in the same manner it was first published to preserve its original nature. Any marks or number seen are left intentionally to preserve its true form.

LETTER OF TRANSMITTAL

SMITHSONIAN INSTITUTION,
BUREAU OF AMERICAN ETHNOLOGY,
Washington, D. C., January 4, 1909.

SIR: I have the honor to submit herewith for publication, with your approval, as Bulletin 41 of this Bureau, the report of Dr. Jesse Walter Fewkes on the work of excavation and repair of Spruce-tree cliff-ruin in the Mesa Verde National Park, Colorado. This was undertaken, pursuant to your instructions, under the direction of the Secretary of the Interior, and a résumé of the general results accomplished is published in the latter's annual report for 1907-8. The present paper is more detailed, and deals with the technical archeological results.

It is gratifying to state that Doctor Fewkes was able to complete the work assigned him, and that Spruce-tree House—the largest ruin in Mesa Verde Park with the exception of the Cliff Palace—is now accessible for the first time, in all its features, to those who would view one of the great aboriginal monuments of our country. This is the more important since Spruce-tree House fulfills the requirements of a "type ruin," and since, owing to its situation, it is the cliff-dwelling from which most tourists obtain their first impressions of structures of this character.

Respectfully, yours, W. H. HOLMES, *Chief.*
THE SECRETARY OF THE SMITHSONIAN INSTITUTION,
Washington, D. C.

ANTIQUITIES OF THE MESA VERDE NATIONAL PARK

SPRUCE-TREE HOUSE

By Jesse Walter Fewkes

SITE OF THE RUIN

Spruce-tree House (pls. 1, 2)[1] is situated in the eastern side of Spruce-tree canyon, a spur of Navaho canyon, which at the site of the ruin is about 150 feet deep, with precipitous walls. The canyon ends blindly at the northern extremity, where there is a spring of good water; it is wooded with tall piñons, cedars, and stately spruces, the tops of which in some cases reach from its bed to its rim. The trees predominating on the rim of the canyon are cedars and pines.

The rock out of which the canyon is eroded is sandstone of varying degrees of hardness alternating with layers of coal and shale. The water percolating through this sandstone, on meeting the harder shale, seeps out of the cliffs to the surface. As the water permeates the rock it gradually undermines the harder layers of sandstone, which fall in great blocks, often leaving arches of rock above deep caves. One of these caves is situated at the end of the canyon where the rim rock overhangs the spring, which is filled by water seeping down from above the shale. Another of these caves is that in which Spruce-tree House is situated. Several smaller caves, and ledges of rock harder than that immediately above, serve as sites for small buildings.

The wearing away of the fallen fragments of the cliffs is much hastened by the waterfalls which in time of heavy rains fall over the rim rock, their force being greatly augmented by the height from which the water is precipitated. The fragments continually falling from the roofs of the caves form a talus that extends from the floors of the caves down the side of the cliff. The cliff-dwellings are erected on the top of this talus.

RECENT HISTORY

Although there was once an old Spanish trail winding over the mountains by way of Mancos and Dolores from what is now New Mexico to Utah, the early visitors to this part of Colorado seem not to have been impressed with the prehistoric cliff-houses in the Montezuma valley and on the Mesa Verde; at least they left no accounts of them in their writings. It appears that these early Spanish travelers encountered the Ute, possibly the Navaho Indians, along this trail, but the more peaceable people who built and occupied the villages now ruins in the neighborhood of Mancos and Cortez had apparently disappeared even at that early date. Indian legends regarding the inhabitants of the cliff-dwellings of the Mesa Verde are very limited and indistinct. The Ute designate them as the houses of the dead, or *moki*, the name commonly applied to the Hopi of Arizona. One of the Ute legends mentions the last battle between the ancient house-builders of Montezuma valley and their ancestors, near Battle Rock, in which it is said that the former were defeated and turned into fishes.

The ruins in Mancos canyon were discovered and first explored in 1874 by a Government party under Mr. W. H. Jackson.[2] The walls of ruins situated in the valley have been so long exposed to the weather that they are very much broken down, being practically nothing more than mounds. The few cliff-dwellings in Mancos canyon which were examined by Jackson are for the most part small; these are found on the west side. One of the largest is now known as Jackson ruin.

In the year 1875 Prof. W. H. Holmes, now Chief of the Bureau of American Ethnology, made a trip through Mancos canyon and examined several ruins. He described and figured several cliff-houses overlooked by Jackson and drew attention to the remarkable stone towers which are so characteristic of this region.[3] Professor Holmes secured a small collection of earthenware vessels, generally fragmentary, and also a few objects of shells, bone, and wood, figures and descriptions of which accompany his report. Neither Jackson nor Holmes, however, saw the most magnificent ruins of the Mesa Verde. Had they followed up the side canyon of the Mancos they would have discovered, as stated by Nordenskiöld, "ruins so magnificent that they surpass anything of the kind known in the United States."

The following story of the discovery of the largest two of these ruins, one of which is the subject of this article, is quoted from Nordenskiöld:[4]

> The honour of the discovery of these remarkable ruins belongs to Richard and Alfred Wetherill of Mancos. The family own large herds of cattle, which wander about on the Mesa Verde. The care of these herds often calls for long rides on the mesa and in its labyrinth of cañons. During these long excursions ruins, the one more magnificent than the other, have been discovered. The two largest were found by Richard Wetherill and Charley Mason one December day in 1888, as they were riding together through the piñon wood on the mesa, in search of a stray herd. They had penetrated through the dense scrub to the edge of a deep cañon. In the opposite cliff, sheltered by a huge, massive vault of rock, there lay before their astonished eyes a whole town with towers and walls, rising out of a heap of ruins. This grand monument of bygone ages seemed to

them well deserving of the name of the Cliff Palace. Not far from this place, but in a different cañon, they discovered on the same day another very large cliff-dwelling; to this they gave the name of Sprucetree House, from a great spruce that jutted forth from the ruins. During the course of years Richard and Alfred Wetherill have explored the mesa and its cañons in all directions; they have thus gained a more thorough knowledge of its ruins than anyone. Together with their brothers John, Clayton, and Wynn, they have also carried out excavations, during which a number of extremely interesting finds have been made. A considerable collection of these objects, comprising skulls, pottery, implements of stone, bone, and wood, etc., has been sold to "The Historical Society of Colorado." A still larger collection is in the possession of the Wetherill family. A brief catalogue of this collection forms the first printed notice of the remarkable finds made during the excavations.

Mr. F. H. Chapin visited the Mesa Verde ruins in 1889 and published illustrated accounts[5] of his visit containing much information largely derived from the Wetherills and others. Dr. W. R. Birdsall also published an account of these ruins,[6] illustrated by several figures. Neither Chapin nor Birdsall gives special attention to the ruin now called Spruce-tree House, and while their writings are interesting and valuable in the general history of the archeology of the Mesa Verde, they are of little aid in our studies of this particular ruin. The same may be said of the short and incomplete notices of the Mesa Verde ruins which have appeared in several newspapers. The scientific descriptions of Spruce-tree House as well as of other Mesa Verde ruins begin with the memoir of the talented Swede, Baron Gustav Nordenskiöld, who, in his work, "The Cliff Dwellers of the Mesa Verde", gives the first comprehensive account of the ruins of this mesa. It is not too much to say that he has rendered to American archeology in this work a service which will be more and more appreciated in the future development of that science. In order to make more comprehensive the present author's report on Spruce-tree House, the following description of this ruin is quoted from Nordenskiöld's memoir (pp. 50-56):

> A few hundred paces to the north along the cliff lead to a large cave, in the shadow of which lie the ruins of a whole village, *Sprucetree House*. This cave is 70 m. broad and 28 m. in depth. The height is small in comparison with the depth, the interior of the cave thus being rather dark. The ground is fairly even and lies almost on a level, which has considerably facilitated the building operations. A plan of the ruins is given in Pl. IX. A great part of the house, or rather village, is in an excellent state of preservation, both the walls, which at some places are several stories high and rise to the roof of rock, and the floors between the different stories still remaining. The architecture is the same as that described in the ruins on Wetherill's Mesa.

In some parts more care is perhaps displayed in the shape of the blocks and in the joints between them. The walls, here as in other cliff-dwellings, are about 0.3 m. thick, seldom more. A point which immediately strikes the eye in Pl. IX, is that no premeditated design has been followed in the erection of the buildings. It seems as if only a few rooms had first been built, additions having subsequently been made to meet the requirements of the increasing population. This circumstance, which I have already touched upon when describing other ruins, may be observed in most of the cliff-dwellings. There is further evidence to show that the whole village was not erected at the same time. At several places it may be seen that new walls have been added to the old, though the stones of both walls do not fit into each other, as is the case when two adjacent walls have been constructed simultaneously. The arrangement of the rooms has been determined by the surrounding cliff, the walls being generally built either at right angles or parallel to it. At some places the walls of several adjoining apartments of about equal size have been consistently erected in the same direction, some blocks of rooms thus possessing a regularity which is wanting in the cliff-village as a whole. This is perhaps the first stage in the development of the cliff-dwellings to the villages whose ruins are common in the valleys and on the mesa, and which are constructed according to a fixed design.

In the plan (Pl. IX) it may be seen that the cave contains two distinct groups of rooms. At about the middle of the cliff-village a kind of passage (23), uninterrupted by any wall, runs through the whole ruin. We found the remains, however, of a cross wall projecting from an elliptical room (14 in the plan) in the south part of the village. Each of these two divisions of the ruin contains an open space (16 and 28) at the back of the cave, the ground in both these places being covered with bird droppings. It is probable that this was the place where tame turkeys were kept, though it can not have been a very pleasant abode for them, for at least in the north of the ruin this part of the cave is almost pitch dark, the walls of the inner court (28), rising up to the roof of rock. In each of the two divisions of the cliff-village a number of estufas were built, in the north at least five, in the south at least two; while several more are, no doubt, buried in the heaps of ruins. These estufas preserve to the least detail the ordinary type (diam. 4-5 metres) fully described above. They are generally situated in front of the other rooms, with their foundations sunk deeper in the ground, and have never had an upper story. Even their site suggests that they were used for some special purpose, probably as assembly-rooms at religious festivities held by those members of the tribe who lived in the adjacent rooms. In all the estufas without exception the roof has fallen in. It is probable, as I have mentioned before, that the entrance of these rooms, as is still the case among the Pueblo Indians, was constructed in the roof. The other rooms were entered by narrow doorways (breadth 40-55 cm., height 65-80 cm.). These doorways are generally rectangular, often somewhat narrower at the top; the sill consists, as already described, of a long stone slab, the lintel of a few sticks a couple of centimetres in thickness, laid across the opening to support the wall above them. The arch was unknown to the builders of these villages, even in the form common among the ruins of Central America, and constructed by carrying the walls on both sides of the doorway nearer to each other as each course of stones was laid, until they could be joined by a stone slab placed across them. Along both sides of the doorway and under the lintel a narrow frame of thin sticks covered with plaster was built (see fig. 28 to the left). This frame, which leant inwards, served to support the door, a thin, flat, rectangular stone slab of suitable size. Through two loops on the outside of the wall, made of osiers inserted in the chinks between the stones, and placed one on each side of the doorway, a thin stick was passed, thus forming a kind of bolt. Besides this type of door most cliff-villages contain examples of another. Some doorways present the appearance shown in fig. 28 to the right (height 90 cm., breadth at the top, 45 cm., at the bottom 30 cm.) They were not closed with a stone slab. They probably belonged to the rooms most frequented in daily life, and were therefore fashioned so as to admit of more convenient ingress and egress. The other doorways, through which it is by no means easy to enter, probably belonged in general to storerooms or other chambers not so often visited and requiring for some reason or other a door to close them. It should be mentioned that the large, **T**-shaped doors described above are rare in the ruins on Wetherill's Mesa which both in architecture and in other respects bear traces of less care and skill on the part of the builders, and are also in a more advanced stage of decay, thus giving the impression of greater age than the ruins treated of in the present chapter, though without showing any essential differences.

The rooms, with the exception of the estufas, are nearly always rectangular, the sides measuring seldom more than two or three metres. North of the passage (23) which divides the ruin into two parts, a whole series of rooms (26, 29-33) still extends outwards from the back of the cave, their walls reaching up to the roof of rock, and the floors between the upper and lower stories being in a perfect state of preservation. The lower rooms are generally entered by small doors opening directly on the "street." In the interior the darkness is almost complete, especially in room 34, which has no direct communication with the passage. It must be approached either through 35, which is a narrow room with the short side towards the "street" entirely open, or through 33. We used 34 as a dark room for photographic purposes.

The walls and roof of some rooms are thick with soot. The inhabitants must have had no great pretensions as regards light and air. The doorways served also as windows, though at one or two places small, quadrangular loop-holes have been constructed in the walls for the passage of light. Entrance to the upper story is generally gained by a small quadrangular hole in the roof at a corner of the lower room, a foothold being afforded merely by some stones projecting from the walls. This hole was probably covered with a stone slab like the doors. Thick beams of cedar or piñon and across them thin poles, laid close together, form the floors between the stories. In some cases long sticks were laid in pairs across the cedar beams at a distance of some decimeters between the pairs, a layer of twigs and cedar bast was placed over the sticks, and the whole was covered with clay, which was smoothed and dried.

In several other parts of the ruin besides this the walls still reach the roof of the cave. These walls are marked in the plan. In all the estufas and in some of the other rooms, perhaps the apartments of chiefs or families of rank, the walls are covered with a thin coat of yellow plaster. In one instance they are even decorated with a painting, representing two birds, which is reproduced in one of the following chapters. Pl. X: 2 shows a part of the ruin, situated in the north of the cave. The spot from which the photograph was taken, as well as the approximate angle of view, is marked in the plan. The left half of the photograph is occupied by a wall with doorways, rising to a height of three stories and up to the roof of the cave; within the wall lies a series of five rooms on the ground floor; behind these rooms the large open space mentioned above (28) occupies the depths of the cavern. Here the beams are all that remains of the floors of the upper stories, their ends projecting a foot or two beyond the wall between the second and third stories, where support was probably afforded in this manner to a balcony, as an easier means of communication between the rooms of the upper stories. In front of this part of the building, but not visible in the photograph, lie two estufas and outside the latter is a long wall. To judge by the ruins, the roofs of these estufas once lay on a level with the floors of the adjoining rooms, so that over the estufas, which were sunk in the ground, only the roofs being left visible, the inhabitants had an open space, bounded on the outside by the said long wall, which formed a rampart at the edge of the talus. The same method of construction is employed by the Moki Indians in their estufas; but these rooms are rectangular in form.—Farther north lies another estufa. Its site, nearest to the cliff wall, would seem to indicate that it is the oldest. The walls in the north of the ruin still rise to a height of 6 metres.

The south part of the ruin is similar in all respects to the north. Its only singularity is a room of elliptical shape (axes 3.6 and 2.9 m.); from this room a wall runs south, enclosing a small open space (16) where, as at the corresponding place in the north of the ruin, the ground is covered with bird droppings mixed with dust and refuse. At one end there are two semicircular enclosures (17, 18) of loose stones forming low walls. In a pentagonal room (8) south of this open space one corner contains a kind of closet (height 1.2 m., length and breadth O.9 m.) composed of two large upright slabs of stone, with a third slab laid across them in a sloping position and cemented fast (see fig. 29). Of the use to which this "closet" was put, I am ignorant. Farther south some of the rooms are situated on a narrow ledge, along which a wall has been erected, probably for purposes of defense.

Plate X: 1 is a photograph of Sprucetree House from the opposite side of the cañon. The illustrations give a better idea of the ruin's appearance than any description could do.

Our excavations in Sprucetree House lasted only a few days. This ruin will certainly prove a rich field for future researches.[7] Some handsome baskets and pieces of pottery were the best finds made during the short period of our excavations. In a room (69) belonging to the north part of the ruin we found the skeletons of three children who had been buried there.

A circumstance which deserves mention, and which was undoubtedly of great importance to the inhabitants of Sprucetree House, is the presence at the bottom of the cañon, a few hundred paces from the ruin, of a fairly good spring.

Near Sprucetree House there are a number of very small, isolated rooms, situated on ledges most difficult of access. One of these tiny cliff-dwellings may be seen to the left in fig. 27. It is improbable that these cells, which are sometimes so small that one can hardly turn in them, were really dwelling places; their object is unknown to me, unless it was one of defense, archers being posted there when danger threatened, so that the enemy might have to face a volley of arrows from several points at once. In such a position a few men could defend themselves, even against an enemy of superior force, for an assailant could reach the ledge only by climbing with hands and feet. Another explanation, perhaps better, was suggested to me by Mr. Fewkes. He thinks that these small rooms were shrines where offerings to the gods were deposited. No object has, however, been found to confirm this suggestion.

To the right of fig. 27 a huge spruce may be seen. Its roots lie within the ruins of Sprucetree House, the trunk projecting from the wall of an estufa.

In Pl. X: 1 the tree is wanting. I had it cut down in order to ascertain its age. We counted the rings, which were very distinct, twice over, the results being respectively 167 and 169. I had supposed from the thickness of the tree that the number of the rings was much greater.

GENERAL FEATURES

Like the majority of cliff-dwellings in the Mesa Verde National Park, Spruce-tree House stands in a recess protected above by an overhanging cliff. Its form is crescentic, following that of the cave and extending approximately north and south.

The author has given the number of rooms and their dimensions in his report to the Secretary of the Interior (published in the latter's report for 1907-8) from which he makes the following quotation:

> The total length of Spruce-tree House was found to be 216 feet, its width at the widest part 89 feet. There were counted in the Spruce-tree House 114 rooms, the majority of which were secular, and 8 ceremonial chambers or kivas. Nordenskiöld numbered 80 of the former and 7 of the latter, but in this count he apparently did not differentiate in the former those of the first, second and third stories. Spruce-tree House was in places 3 stories high; the third-story rooms had no artificial roof, but the wall of the cave served that purpose. Several rooms, the walls of which are now two stories high, formerly had a third story above the second, but their walls have now fallen, leaving as the only indication of their former union with the cave lines destitute of smoke on the top of the cavern. Of the 114 rooms, at least 14 were uninhabited, being used as storage and mortuary chambers. If we eliminate these from the total number of rooms we have 100 enclosures which might have been dwellings. Allowing 4 inhabitants for each of these 100 rooms would give about 400 persons as an aboriginal population of Spruce-tree House. But it is probable that this estimate should be reduced, as not all the 100 rooms were inhabited at the same time, there being evidence that several of them had occupants long after others were deserted. Approximately, Spruce-tree House had a population not far from 350 people, or about 100 more than that of Walpi, one of the best-known Hopi pueblos.[8]

In the rear of the houses are two large recesses used for refuse-heaps or for burial of the dead. From the abundance of guano and turkey bones it is supposed that turkeys were kept in these places for ceremonial or other purposes. Here have been found several desiccated human bodies commonly called mummies.

The ruin is divided by a street into two sections, the northern and the southern, the former being the more extensive. Light is prevented from entering the larger of these recesses by rooms which reach the roof of the cave. In front of these rooms are circular subterranean rooms called *kivas*, which are sunken below the surrounding level places, or plazas, the roofs of these kivas having been formerly level with the plazas.

The front boundary of these plazas is a wall[9] which when the excavations were begun was buried under débris of fallen walls, but which formerly stood several feet above the level of the plazas.

MAJOR ANTIQUITIES

Under this term are included those immovable prehistoric remains which, taken together, constitute a cliff-dwelling. The architectural features—walls of rooms and structures connected with them, as beams, balconies, fireplaces—are embraced in the term "major antiquities." None of these can be removed from their sites without harm, so they must be protected in the place where they now stand.

In a valuable article on the ruins in valley of the San Juan and its tributaries, Dr. T. Mitchell Prudden[10] recognizes in this region what he designates a "unit type;" that is, a ruin consisting of a kiva backed by a row of rooms generally situated on its north side, with lateral extensions east and west, and a burial place on the opposite, or south, side of the kiva. This form of "unit type," as he points out, is more apparent in ruins situated in an open country than in those built in cliffs. The same form may be recognized in Spruce-tree House, which is composed of several "unit types" arranged side by side. The simplicity of these "unit types" is somewhat modified, however, in this as in all cliff-dwellings, by the form of the site. The author would amend Prudden's definition of the "unit type" as applied to cliff-houses by adding to the latter's description a bounding wall connecting the two lateral extensions of the row of rooms, thus forming the south side of the enclosure of the kiva. For obvious reasons, in this amended description the burial place is absent, as it does not occur in the position assigned to it in the original description.

PLAZAS AND COURTS

As before stated, the buildings of Spruce-tree House are divided into a northern and a southern section by a street which penetrates from plaza G to the rear of the cave. (Pl. 1.) The northern section is not only the larger, but there is evidence that it is also the older. It is bounded by some of the best-constructed buildings, situated along the north side of the street. The rooms of the southern section are less numerous, although in some respects more instructive.

There are practically the same number of plazas as of kivas in this ruin. With the exception of C and D, each plaza is occupied by a single kiva, the roof of which constitutes the central part of the floor of the square enclosure (plaza). The plazas commonly contain remnants of small shrines, fireplaces, and corn-grinding bins, and are perforated by mysterious holes evidently used in ceremonies. Their floors are hardened by the tramping of the many feet that passed over them. The best preserved of all the plazas is that which contains kiva G. It can hardly be supposed that the roof of kiva A served as a dance place, which is the ordinary office of a plaza, but it may have been used in ceremonies. The largest plaza of the series, in the rear of which are rooms while the front is inclosed by the bounding wall, is that containing kivas C and D. The appearance of this plaza before and after clearing out and repairing is shown in plate 3; the view was taken from the north end of the ruin.

From the number of fireplaces and similar evidences it may be concluded that the street already mentioned as dividing the village into two sections served many purposes. Most important of these was its use as the open-air dwellings of the villagers. Its hardened clay floor suggests the constant passage of many feet. Its surface slopes gradually downward from the back of the cave, ending at a step near the round room in the rear of kiva G. This step marks also the eastern boundary of the plaza (G) which contains the best preserved of all the ceremonial rooms of Spruce-tree House.

The discovery by excavation of the wall that originally formed the front of the village was important. In this way was revealed a correct ground plan of the ruin (pl. 1) which had never before been traced by archeologists. When the work began, this wall was deeply buried under accumulated débris, its course not being visible to any considerable extent. By removing the fallen stones composing the débris the wall could be readily traced. In the repair work the original stones were replaced in the structure. As in the first instance this wall was probably about as high as the head, it may have been used for protection. The only openings are small rectangular orifices, the presence of one opposite the external opening of the air flue of each kiva suggesting that formerly these flues opened outside the wall. Two kivas, B and F, are situated west of this wall and therefore outside the village. There are evidences of a walk on top of the talus along the front of the pueblo outside the front wall, and of a retaining wall to prevent the edge of the talus from wearing away. (Pls. 4, 5.)

CONSTRUCTION OF WALLS

The walls of Spruce-tree House were built of stones generally laid in mortar but sometimes piled on one another, the joints being pointed later. Sections of walls in which no mortar was used occur on the **tops of** other walls. These dry walls served among other purposes to shield the roofs of adjacent buildings from snow and rain. Whenever mortar was used it appears that a larger quantity was employed than was necessary, the effect being to weaken the wall since the pointing washed out quickly, being less capable than stone of resisting erosion. When the mortar wore away, the wall was left in danger of falling of its own weight. The pointing was generally done with the hands, the superficial impressions of which show in several places. Small flakes of stone or fragments of pottery were sometimes inserted in the joints, serving both as a decoration, and as a protection by preventing the rapid wearing away of the mortar. Little pellets of clay were also used in the joints for the same purpose.

The character of masonry in different rooms varies considerably, in some places showing good, in others poor, workmanship. As a rule the construction of the corners is weak, the stones forming them being rarely bonded or tied. Component stones of the walls seldom break joints; thus a well-known device by means of which walls are strengthened is lacking, and consequently cracks are numerous and the work is unstable. Fully half the stones used in construction were hammered or dressed into desirable shapes, the remainder being laid as they were gathered, with their flat surfaces exposed when possible. (Pls. 6, 7.)

Some of the walls were out of plumb when constructed and the faces of many were never straight. The walls show evidences of having been repeatedly repaired, as indicated by a difference in color of the mortar used.

Plasters of different colors, as red, white, yellow, and brown, were used. The lower half of the wall of a room was generally painted brownish red, the upper half often white. There are evidences of several coats of plastering, especially on the walls of the kivas, some of which are much discolored with smoke.

The replastering of the walls of Hopi kivas is an incident of the *Powamû* festival, or ceremonial purification of the fields commonly called the "Bean planting," which occurs every February. On a certain day of this festival girls thoroughly replaster the four walls of the kivas and at the close of the work leave impressions of their hands in white mud on the kiva beams.

The rooms of Spruce-tree House may be considered under two headings: secular rooms, and ceremonial rooms, or kivas. The former are rectangular, the latter circular, in form.

SECULAR ROOMS

The secular rooms are the more numerous in Spruce-tree House. In order to designate them in future descriptions they were numbered from 1 to 71, in black paint, in conspicuous places on the walls. ([Pl. 1.](#)) This enumeration begins at the north end and passes thence to the south end of the ruin, but in one or two instances this order is not followed. The author has given below a brief reference to some of the important secular rooms in the series.

The foundations of room 1 were apparently built on a fallen bowlder, the entrance being reached by means of a series of stone steps built into the side hill. The floor of this room is on the level of the second story of other rooms, being continuous with the top of kiva A. It is probable that when this kiva was constructed it was found impossible to make it subterranean on account of the solid rock. A retaining wall was built outside the kiva and the intervening space was filled with earth in order to impart to the room a subterranean character.

Room 2 has three stories, or tiers, of rooms. The floor of the second story, which is the roof of the first, is well preserved, the sides of the hatchway, or means of passage from one room to the one below it, being almost entire. This room possesses a feature which is unique. The base of its south wall is supported by curved timbers, whose ends rest on walls, while the middle is supported by a pillar of masonry. (Pl. 8.) The **T**-shaped door in this wall faces south. It is difficult to understand how the aperture could have been of any use as a doorway unless there was a balcony below it, and no sign of such structure is now visible. The west wall of rooms 2 and 3 was built on top of a fallen rock from which it rises precipitously to a considerable height. The floor of room 4, which lies in front of kiva A, is on a level with the roof of the kiva, and somewhat higher than the surface of the neighboring plaza but not higher than the roof of the first story. As the floors of room 1 and room 4 are on the same level, it would appear that both were considerably elevated or so constructed otherwise that the kiva should be subterranean. This endeavor to render the kiva subterranean by building up around it, when conditions made it impossible to excavate in the solid rock, is paralleled in some other Mesa Verde ruins.

The ventilator of kiva A, as will be seen later, does not open through the front wall, as is usually the case, but on one side. This is accounted for by the presence of a room on this side of the kiva. Rooms 2, 3, 4 were constructed after the walls of kiva A were built, hence several modifications were necessary in the prescribed plan of building these rooms.

The foundation of the inclosure, 5, conforms on one side to the outer wall of the village, and on the other to the curvature of kiva B. As this inclosure does not seem ever to have been roofed, it is probable that it was not a house. A fireplace at one end indicates that cooking was formerly done here. It is instructive to note that the front wall of the ruin begins at this place.

Rooms 6, 7, 8, which lie side by side, closely resemble one another, having much in common. They were evidently dwellings, and may have been sleeping-places for families. Rooms 7 and 8 were two stories high, the floor of no. 8 being on a level with the adjoining plaza. Room 9 is so unusual in its construction that it can not be regarded as a living room. It was used as a mortuary chamber, evidences being strong that it was opened from time to time for new interments. Room 12 also was a ceremonial chamber, and, like the preceding, will be considered later at greater length. The walls of the two rooms, 10 and 11, are low, projecting into plaza C, of whose border they form a part. Near them, or in one corner of the same plaza, is a bin, the sides of which are formed of stone slabs set on edge. The use of this bin is problematical.

The front wall of room 15 had been almost wholly destroyed before the repair work began, and was so unstable that it was necessary to erect a buttress to support it. This room, which is one story high, is irregular in shape; its doorways open into rooms 14 and 16. The walls of rooms 16 and 18 extend to the roof of the cave, shutting out the light on one side from the great refuse-place in the rear of the cliff-dwellings. The openings through the walls of these rooms into this darkened area have been much broken by vandals, and the walls greatly damaged. Room 17, like 16 and 18, is somewhat larger than most of the apartments in Spruce-tree House.

Theoretically it may be supposed that when Spruce-tree House was first settled it had one clan occupying a cluster of rooms, 1-11, and one ceremonial room, kiva A. As the place grew three other "unit types" centering about kivas C-H were added, and still later each of these units was enlarged and new kivas were built in each section. Thus A was enlarged by addition of B; C by addition of D; E by addition of F; and G was subordinated to H. In this way the rooms near the kivas grew in numbers. The block of rooms designated 50-53 is not accounted for, however, in this theory.

Rooms numbered 19-22 are instructive. Their walls are well preserved and form the east side of plaza C. These walls extend from the level of the plaza to the top of the cavern, and in places show some of the best masonry in Spruce-tree House. Just in front of room 19, situated on the left-hand side as one enters the doorway, is a covered recess, where probably ceremonial bread was baked or otherwise cooked. This place bears a strong resemblance to recesses found in Hopi villages, especially as in its floor is set a cooking-pot made of earthenware. Rooms 19-21 are two stories high; there are fireplaces in the corners and doorways on the front sides. The upper stories were approached and entered by balconies. The holes in which formerly rested the beams that supported these balconies can be clearly seen.

Rooms 21 and 22 are three stories high, the entrances to the three tiers being seen in the accompanying view (pl. 6). The beams that once supported the balcony of the third story resemble those of the first story; they project from the wall that forms the front of room 29.

The external entrance to room 24 opens directly on the plaza. Some of the rafters of this room still remain, and near the rear door is a projecting wall, in the corner of which is a fireplace. Although room 25 is three stories high, it does not reach to the cave top. None of the roofs of the rooms one over another are intact, and the west side of the second and third stories is very much broken. The plaster of the second-story walls is decorated with mural paintings that will be considered more fully under Pictographs. It is not evident how entrance through the doorway of the second story was made unless we suppose that there was a notched log, or ladder, for that purpose resting on the ground. In order to strengthen the north wall of room 25 it was braced against the walls of outer rooms by constructing masonry above the doorway that leads from plaza D to room 26. This tied all three walls together and imparted corresponding strength to the whole.

The lower-story walls of room 26 are in fairly good condition, having needed but little repair. There is a good fireplace in the floor at the northeast corner. Excavations revealed a passageway from kiva D into room 26, the opening into the upper room being situated near its north wall. The west wall of room 26 is curved. The walls of rooms 27 and 28 are much dilapidated, the portion of the western section that remains being continuous with the front wall of the pueblo. A small mural fragment ending blindly arises from the outside of the west wall of room 27. This is believed to have been part of a small enclosure used for cooking purposes. Much repairing was necessary in the walls of rooms 27 and 28, since they were situated almost directly in the way of torrents of water which in time of rains fall over the rim of the canyon.

The block of rooms numbered 30-44, situated east of kiva E, have the most substantial masonry and are the best constructed of any in Spruce-tree House. (Pl. 9.) As room 45 is only a dark passageway it should be considered more a street than a dwelling. Rooms 30-36 are one story each in height, rectangular in shape, roofless, and of about the same dimensions; of these room 35 is perhaps the best preserved, having well-constructed fireplaces in one corner. Rooms 37, 38, 39 are built deep in the cavern; their walls, especially those of 38, are very much broken down. There would seem to be hardly a possibility that these rooms were inhabited, especially after the construction of the rooms in front of the cave which shut off all light. But they may easily have served as storage places. Their walls were **constr**ucted of well-dressed stones and afford an example of good masonry work.

Here and there are indications of other rooms in the darker parts of the cave. In some instances their walls extended to the roof of the cave where their former position is indicated by light bands on the sooty surface.

Rooms 40-47 are among the finest chambers in Spruce-tree House. Rooms 48 and 49 are very much damaged, the walls having fallen, leaving only the foundations above the ground level. Several rooms in this part of the ruin, especially rooms 43 (pl. 9) and 44, still have roofs and floors as well preserved as when they were built, and although dark, owing to lack of windows, they have fireplaces in the corners, the smoke escaping apparently through the diminutive door openings. The thresholds of some of the doorways are too high above the main court to be entered without ladders or notched poles, but projecting stones or depressions for the feet, still visible, apparently assisted the inhabitants, as they do modern visitors, to enter rooms 41 and 42.

Each of the small block of rooms 50-53 is one story and without a roof, but possessing well-preserved ground floors. In room 53 there is a depression in the floor at the bottom of which is a small hole.[11]

In the preceding pages there have been considered the rooms of the north section of Spruce-tree House, embracing dwellings, ceremonial rooms, and other enclosures north of the main court, and the space in the rear called the refuse-heap—in all, six circular ceremonial rooms and a large majority of the living and storage rooms. From all the available facts at the author's disposal it is supposed that this portion is older than the south section, which contains but two ceremonial rooms and not more than a third the number of secular dwellings.[12]

The cluster of rooms connected with kivas G and H shows signs of having been built by a clan which may have joined Spruce-tree House subsequent to the construction of the north section of the village. The ceremonial rooms in this section differ in form from the others. Here occur two round rooms or towers, duplicates of which have not been found in the north section.

Room 61 in the south section of Spruce-tree House has a closet made of flat stones set on edge and covered with a perforated stone slab slightly inclined from the horizontal.

The inclosures at the extreme south end, which follow a narrow ledge, appear to have been unroofed passages rather than rooms. On **ledges** somewhat higher there are small granaries each with a hole in the side, probably for the storage of corn.

It will be noticed that the terraced form of buildings, almost universal in modern three-story pueblos and common in pictures of ruins south of the San Juan, does not exist in Spruce-tree House. The front of the three tiers of rooms 22, 23, as shown in plate 3, is vertical, not terraced from foundation to top. Whether the walls of rooms now in ruins were terraced or not can not be determined, for these have been washed out and have fallen to so great an extent that it is almost impossible to tell their original form. Rooms 25-28, for instance, might have been terraced on the front side, but it is more reasonable to suppose they were not;[13] from the arrangement of doors it would seem that there was a lateral entrance on the ground floor rather than through roofs.

BALCONIES

Balconies attached to the walls of buildings below rows of doors occurred at several places. On no other hypothesis than the presence of these structures can be explained the elevated situation of entrances opening into the rooms immediately above rooms 20, 21, 22. In fact, there appear to have been two balconies at this place, one above the other, but all now left of them is the projecting floor-beams, and a fragment of a floor on the projections at the north end of the lower one, in front of room 20. These balconies (pl. 3) were apparently constructed in the same way as the structure that gives the name to the ruin called Balcony House; they seem to have been used by the inhabitants as a means of communication between neighboring rooms.

Nordenskiöld writes:[14]

> The second story is furnished along the wall just mentioned, with a balcony; the joists between the two stories project a couple of feet, long poles lie across them parallel to the walls, the poles are covered with a layer of cedar bast, and, finally with dried clay.

FIREPLACES

There are many fireplaces in Spruce-tree House, in rooms, plazas, and courts. From their number it is evident that most of the cooking must have been done by the ancients in the courts and plazas, rather than in the houses. The rooms are so small and so poorly ventilated that it would not be possible for any one to remain in them when fires are burning.

The top of the cave in which Spruce-tree House is built is covered with soot, showing that formerly there were many fires in the courts and other open places of the village. In almost every corner of the buildings in which a fire could be made the effect of smoke on the adjoining walls is discernible, while ashes are found in a depression in the floor. These fireplaces are very simple, consisting simply of square box-like structures bounded by a few flat stones set on edge. In other instances a depression in the floor bordered with a low ridge of adobe served as a fireplace. There remains nothing to indicate that the inhabitants were familiar with chimneys or firehoods as is the case among the modern pueblos. Certain small rooms suggest cook-houses, or places where *piki*, or paper bread, was fried by the women on slabs of stone over a fire, but none of these slabs were found in place. The fireplaces of the kivas are considered specially in an account of the structure of those rooms (see p. 18).

No evidence that Spruce-tree House people burnt coal was observed, although they were familiar with lignite and seams of coal underlie their mesa.

DOORS AND WINDOWS

There are both doors and windows in the secular houses of Spruce-tree House, although the two rarely exist together. The windows, most of which are small square peep-holes or round orifices, look obliquely downward, as if their purpose was rather for outlook than for air, the latter being admitted as a rule through the doorway. (Pls. 10, 11.)

The two types of doorways differ more in shape than in any other feature. These types may be called the rectangular and the **T**-shaped form. Both are found at a high level, but it can not be discovered how they could have been entered without ladders or notched logs. Although these modes of entrance were apparently often used it is remarkable that no traces of the logs have yet been found in the extensive excavations at Spruce-tree House. The **T**-shaped doorways are often filled in at the lower or narrow part, sometimes with stones rudely placed, oftentimes with good masonry, by which a **T**-shaped door is converted into one of square type. Doorways of both types are often completely filled in, leaving only their outlines on the sides of the wall.

FLOORS AND ROOFS

The floors of the rooms are all smoothly plastered and, although purposely broken through in places by those in search of specimens, are otherwise in fairly good condition. In one of the rooms at the left of the main court is a small round hole at the bottom of a concave depression like a fireplace, the use of which is not known. Many of the floors sound hollow when struck, but this fact is not an indication of the presence of cavities below. In tiers of rooms that rise above the first story the roof of one room forms the floor of the room above it. Wherever roofs still remain they are found to be well constructed (pl. 9) and to resemble those of the old Hopi houses. In Spruce-tree House the roofs are supported by timbers laid from one wall to another; these in turn support crossbeams on which were placed layers of cedar bark covered with a thick coating of mud. In several roofs hatchways are still to be seen, but in most cases entrances are at the sides. One second-story room has a fireplace constructed like those on the ground floor or on the roof. Several fireplaces were found on the roofs of buildings one story high.

The largest slabs of stone used in the construction of the rooms of Spruce-tree House were generally made into lintels and thresholds. The latter surfaces were often worn smooth by those crawling through the opening and in some cases they show grooves for the insertion of the door slabs. Although the sides of the door are often upright slabs of stone these may be replaced by boards set in adobe plaster. Similar split boards often form lintels.

The door was apparently a flat stone set in an adobe casing on the inside of the frame where it was held in position by a stick. Each end of this stick was inserted into an eyelet made of bent osiers firmly set in the wall. Many of these broken eyelets can still be seen in the doorways and one or two are still entire. A slab of stone closing one of the doorways is still in place.

KIVAS

There are eight circular subterranean rooms identified as ceremonial rooms, or *kivas*, in Spruce-tree House (pls. 12, 13). Beginning on the north these kivas are designated by letters A-H. When excavation began small depressions full of fallen stones, with here and there a stone buttress projecting out of the débris, were the only indications of the sites of these important chambers. The walls of kiva H were the most dilapidated and the most obscured of all, the central portion of the front wall of rooms 62 and 63 having fallen into this chamber; added to the débris were the high walls of the round room, no. 69. Kiva G is the best-preserved kiva and kiva A the most exceptional in construction. Kiva B, never seen by previous **inves**tigators, was in poor condition, its walls being almost completely broken down. Part of the wall of kiva A is double (pl. 13), indicating a circular room built inside another room the shape of which inclines to oval, the former utilizing a portion of the wall of the latter. This kiva is also exceptional in being surrounded on three sides by rooms, the fourth side being the wall of the cavern. From several considerations the author regards this as the oldest kiva in Spruce-tree House.

The typical structure of a Spruce-tree House kiva is as follows: Its form is circular or oval; the site is subterranean, the roof being level with the floor of the surrounding plaza. (Pls. 13-15.) Two walls, an outer and an inner, inclose the room, the latter forming the lower part. Upon the top of this lower wall rest six pedestals, which support the roof beams; the outer wall braces these pedestals on one side. The spaces between these pedestals form recesses in which the floors extend a few feet above the floor of the room.

The floor of the kiva is generally plastered, but in some cases is solid rock. The fireplace is a circular depression in the floor, its purpose being indicated by the wood ashes found therein. Its lining is ordinarily made of clay, which in some instances is replaced by stones set on edge.

The other important opening in the floor is one called *sipapû*, or symbolic opening into the underworld. This is generally situated near the center of the room, opposite the fireplace. This opening into the underworld is barely large enough to admit the human hand and extends only about a foot below the floor surface. It is commonly single, but in one kiva two of these orifices were detected. A similar symbolic opening occurs in modern Hopi kivas, as has been repeatedly described in the author's accounts of pueblo ceremonials. An important structure of a Spruce-tree House kiva is an upright slab of rock, or a narrow thin wall of masonry, placed between the fireplace and the wall of the kiva. This object, sometimes called an altar, serves as a deflector, its function being to distribute the air which enters the kiva at the floor level through a vertical shaft, or ventilator. Every kiva has at least one such deflector, a single fireplace, and the sipapû, or ceremonial opening mentioned above.

Several small cubby-holes, or receptacles for paint or small ceremonial objects, generally occur in the lower walls of the kiva. In addition to these there exist openings ample in size to admit the human body, which serve different purposes. The first kind communicate directly with passageways through which one can pass from the kiva into a neighboring room or plaza. Such a passageway in kiva E has steps near the opening in the floor of room 35. This entrance is not believed, however, to be the only way by which one could enter or leave this room, but was a private passage, the main **entran**ce being through the roof. Another lateral passageway is found in kiva D, where there is an opening in the south wall communicating with the open air by means of an exit in the floor of room 26; another opening is found in the wall on the east side. Kiva C has a lateral opening communicating with a vertical passageway which opens in the middle of the neighboring plaza. In addition to lateral openings all kivas without exception have others that serve as ventilators, as before mentioned, by which air is introduced on the floor level of the kivas. The opening of this kind communicates through a horizontal passage with a vertical flue which finds its way outside the room on a level with the roof. In cases where the kiva is situated near the front wall these ventilators open through this wall by means of square apertures. All ventilator openings are in the west wall except that of kiva A, which is the only one that has rooms on that side.

The construction of kiva roofs must have been a difficult problem (pls. 14, 15). The beams (L-1 to L-4) are supported by the six pedestals (C) which stand upon the banquettes (A), and in turn are supported by the outer wall (B) of the kiva. On top of each of these pedestals is inserted a short stick (H) that served as a peg on which the inmates hung their ceremonial paraphernalia. The supports of the roof were cedar logs cut in suitable lengths by stone axes. Three logs were laid, connecting adjacent pedestals upon which they rested. These logs, which were large enough to support considerable weight, had been stripped of their bark. Upon these six beams were laid an equal number of beams, spanning the intervals between those first placed, as shown in the illustration (pl. 15). Upon the last-mentioned beams were still other logs extending across the kiva, as also shown in the plate.

The main weight of the roof was supported by two large logs which extended diametrically across the kiva from one wall to the wall opposite; they were placed a short distance apart, parallel with each other. The distance between these logs determines the width of the doorway, two sides of which they form. The other two sides are formed by two beams (L-4) of moderate size, laid across these logs, the space between them and the two beams being filled in with other logs, forming a compact framework. No nails are necessary in a roof constructed in this way.

The smaller interstices between the logs were filled in with small sticks and twigs, thus preventing soil from dropping into the room. Over the supports of the roof was spread a layer of cedar bark (M) covered with mud (N), laid deep enough to bring the top of the roof to the level of the plaza in which the kiva is situated.

No kiva was found in which the plastering of the walls was supported by sticks, as sometimes occurs here, according to Nordenskiöld, **and in** one or more of the Hopi kivas. The plastering of the walls was placed directly on the masonry.

It is probable that the kiva walls were painted with various devices before their roofs fell in and other mutilation of the walls took place. Among these designs parallel lines in white were common. Similar lines are still made with meal on kiva walls in Hopi ceremonies, as the author has often described. One of the pedestals of kiva A is decorated with a triangular figure on the margin of the dado, to which reference will be made later.

The author has found no conclusive answer to the question why the kivas are built under ground and are circular in form. He believes both conditions to be survivals of ancient "pit-houses," or subterranean dwellings of an antecedent people. In this explanation the kiva is regarded as the oldest form of building in the cliff-dwellings. We have the authority of observation bearing on this point. Pit-dwellings are recorded from several ruins. In a recent work Dr. Walter Hough figures and describes certain dwellings of subterranean character that are sometimes found in clusters,[15] while the present author has observed subterranean rooms so situated as to leave no doubt of their great antiquity.[16]

The form of the kiva is characteristic and may be used as a basis of classification of pueblo culture. The people whose kivas are circular inhabited villages now ruins in the valley of the San Juan and its tributaries, in Chelly canyon, Chaco canyon, and on the western plateau of the Rio Grande.

The rectangular kiva is a structure altogether different from a round kiva, morphologically, genetically, and geographically. It is peculiar to the southern and western pueblo area, and while of later growth, should not be regarded as an evolution from the circular kiva. Several authors have found in circular kivas survivals of nomadic architectural conditions, while the position of these rooms, in nearly every instance in front of the other rooms of the cliff-dwelling, has led others to accept the theory that they were later additions to the village, which should be ascribed to a different race. It would seem that this hypothesis hardly conforms to facts, as some kivas have secular rooms in front of them which show evidences of later construction. The strongest objection to the theory that kivas are modified houses of nomads is the style of roof construction.

Kiva A

This room (pl. 13), which is the most northerly of all of the ceremonial rooms of Spruce-tree House, is, the author believes, the **oldest**. In construction this is a remarkable chamber. It is built directly under the cliff, which forms part of its walls. In addition to its site the remarkable features are its double walls, and its floor on the level of the roofs of the other kivas. Although this kiva is not naturally subterranean, the earth and walls built up around it make it to all intents below the surface of the ground.

It appears from the arrangement of walls and banquettes that there is here presented an example of one room constructed inside of another, the inner room utilizing for its wall a portion of the outer. The inner room is more nearly circular than the outer in which it was subsequently built. In this inner room as in other kivas there are six banquettes, and the same number of pedestals to support the roof. Three of these pedestals are common to both rooms. The floor of this room shows nothing peculiar. It has a fire hole, a sipapû, and a deflector, or low wall between the fire hole and the entrance into the horizontal passageway of the ventilator. The ventilator itself opens just outside the west wall through a passageway, the walls of which stand on the wall of a neighboring room. No plaza of any considerable size surrounded the top of this kiva.

In order to get an idea as to how many rectangular rooms naturally accompany a single kiva, the author examined the ground plans of such cliff-dwellings as are known to have but one circular kiva, the majority of these being in the Chelly canyon. While it was not possible to determine the point satisfactorily, it was found that in several instances the circular kiva lies in the middle of several rooms, a fact which would seem to indicate that it was built first and that the square rooms were added later. Several clusters of rooms, each cluster having one kiva, closely resemble kiva A and its surroundings, in both form and structure.

Kiva B

The walls of this subterranean room had escaped all previous observers. They are very much dilapidated, being wholly concealed when work of excavation began. A large old cedar tree growing in the middle of this room led the author to abandon its complete excavation, which promised little return either in enlarging our knowledge of the ground plan of Spruce-tree House or in shedding additional light on the culture of its prehistoric inhabitants.

Kivas C and D

The two kivas, C and D, the roofs of which form the greater part of plaza C, logically belong together in our consideration. One of these rooms, C, was roofed over by the author, who followed as a model the roofs of the two kivas of the House with the Square Tower (Peabody House); the other shows a few log supports of an original roof—the only Spruce-tree House kiva of which this is true.

Not only was the roof of the kiva restored but its walls were well repaired, so that it now presents all the essential features of an ancient kiva. On one of the banquettes of this room the author found a vase which was evidently a receptacle for pigments or other ceremonial paraphernalia.

Kiva D has a passageway leading into room 26 and a second opening in the west wall on the floor level, besides a ventilator of the type common to all kivas. The top of the opening in the west wall appears covered with a flat stone in one of the photographic views (plate 11).

The wall in front of the village in the neighborhood of kivas C and D was wholly concealed by débris when work was begun on this part of the ruin. Excavation of this débris showed that opposite each kiva there was an opening with which the ventilator is believed formerly to have been connected. There seems to have been a low-storied house, possibly a cooking-place, provided with a roof, in an interval between kivas C and D; in the floor of the plaza at this point a well-made fire hole was uncovered.

Kiva E

Kiva E is one of the finest which was excavated, showing all the typical structures of these characteristic rooms; it almost fills the plaza in which it is situated. The exceptional feature of this room is a passageway through the west wall. Room 35 may have been the house of a chief or of a priest who kept in it his masks or other ceremonial paraphernalia. A similar opening in the wall of one of the Hopi kivas communicates with a dark room in which are kept altars and other ceremonial objects. When such a passageway into a dark chamber is not in use it is closed by a slab of stone.

Kiva F

Kiva F might be designated the Spruce-tree kiva from the large spruce tree that formerly grew near its outer wall. Its stump is now visible, but the tree lies extended in the canyon.

The walls of this kiva were poorly preserved, and only two of the pedestals were in place. The walls were repaired and the roof restored. This room is situated outside the walls, and in that respect recalls kiva B, described above. The ventilator opening of this kiva is situated on the south instead of on the west side of the room, as is the rule in other kivas. The large size of this room would indicate that it was of great importance in the religious ceremonials of the prehistoric inhabitants of Spruce-tree House, but all indications point to its late construction.[17]

Kiva G

Kiva G was so well preserved that its walls were thoroughly restored; it now stands as typical of one of these rooms in which the several characteristic features may be seen. For the guidance of visitors, letters or numbers accompanied by explanatory labels were painted by the author on the walls of the kiva.

Kiva G lies just below and in front of the round tower of Spruce-tree House, which is situated in the neighborhood of the main court, and may therefore be looked on as one of the most important kivas in the cliff-dwelling.[18] The solid stone floor of this room had been cut down about 8 inches.

Kiva H

Kiva H, the largest in Spruce-tree House, contained some of the best specimens excavated by the author. Its shape is oval rather than circular, and it fills the whole space inclosed by walls of rooms on three sides. In the neighborhood of kiva H is a comparatively spacious plaza which is bounded on the front by a low wall, now repaired, and on the other sides are high rooms. The plaza containing this kiva was ample for ceremonial dances which undoubtedly formerly occurred in it. The walls of kiva H formerly had a marked pinkish color, showing no sign of blackening by smoke except in places. Charred roof beams were excavated at one place, however, and charcoal occurred deep under the débris that filled this room.

CIRCULAR ROOMS OTHER THAN KIVAS

There are two rooms (nos. 54, 69) of circular shape in Spruce-tree House, one of which resembles the "tower" in the Cliff Palace. This room (no. 54) is situated to the right hand of the main court above referred to, into which it projects without attachment except on one side. Its walls have two small windows or openings which have been called doorways, and are of a single story in height. This tower was apparently ceremonial in character.

It is instructive to mention that remains of a fire hole containing wood ashes occur in the floor on one side of this room, and that the walls are pierced with several small holes opening at an angle. Only foundations remain of the other circular room. It was situated on the south side of the open space containing kiva H and formed a bastion at the north end of the front wall. The floor of this room was wholly covered with fallen débris and its ground plan was wholly concealed when the excavations began; it was only with considerable difficulty that the foundation walls could be traced.

CEREMONIAL ROOM OTHER THAN KIVA

While the circular subterranean rooms above mentioned are believed to be the most common ceremonial chambers, there are others in the cliff-dwellings which were undoubtedly used for similar purposes. One of these, designated room 12, adjoins the mortuary room (11) and opens on the plaza C, D. In some respects the form of this room is similar to an "estufa of singular construction" described and figured in Nordenskiöld's account of Cliff Palace. Certain distinctive characters of this room separate it on one side from a kiva and on the other from a dwelling. In the first place, it lacks the circular form and subterranean site. The six pedestals which universally support the roofs are likewise absent. In fact they are not needed because in this room the top of the cave serves as the roof. A bank extends around three sides of the room, the fourth side being the perpendicular wall of the cliff. In the southeast corner is an opening, which recalls that in the "estufa of singular construction" described by Nordenskiöld.[19]

MORTUARY ROOM

Room 9 may be designated a mortuary room from the fact that at least four human skeletons and accompanying offerings have been found in its floor. Three of those, excavated several years ago, were said to have been infants; the skull of one of these was figured and described by Prof. G. Retzius, in Nordenskiöld's memoir. The skeleton found by the author was that of an adult and was accompanied by mortuary offerings. The skull and some of the larger bones were well preserved.[20] Evidently the doorway of this room had been walled up and there are indications that the burials took place at intervals, the last occurring before the desertion of the village.

The presence of burials in the floors of rooms in Spruce-tree House was to be expected, as the practice of thus disposing of the dead was known from other ruins of the Park, but it has not been pointed out that we have in this region good evidence of several successive interments in the same room. The existence of this intramural burial room in the south end of the ruin is one of the facts that can be adduced pointing to the conclusion that this part of the ruin is very old.

SMALL LEDGE-HOUSES

Not far from the Spruce-tree House, situated in the same canyon, there are small one-room houses perched on narrow ledges situated generally a little higher than the cave containing the main ruin. **Although** it is difficult to enter some of these houses, members of the author's party visited all of them, and two of the workmen slept in a small ledge-house on the west side of the canyon. Except in rare cases these smaller houses can not be considered dwellings; they may have been used for storage, although it is more than likely that they were resorted to by priests when they wished to pray for rain or to perform certain ceremonies. The ledge-houses form a distinct type of ruin; they are rarely multiple-chambered and therefore are not capacious enough for more than one family.

STAIRWAYS

There are two or three old stairway trails in the neighborhood of Spruce-tree House. These consist of a succession of holes for hands and feet, or of a series of pits cut in the face of the cliff at convenient distances. One of these ancient trails is situated on the west side of the canyon not far from the modern trail to the spring; the other lies on the east side a few feet north of the ruin. Both of these trails were appropriately labeled for the convenience of future visitors. There is still another ancient trail along the east canyon wall south of the ruin. Although all these trails are somewhat obscure, it is hoped that they can be readily found by means of the labels posted near them.

REFUSE-HEAPS

In the rear of the buildings are two large open spaces which, from their positions relative to the main street, may be called the northern and southern refuse-heaps. They merit more than passing consideration. The former, being the larger, has not yet been thoroughly cleared out, although pretty well dug over before the repair work was begun. The author completely cleared out the southern refuse-heap and excavated to its floor.[21]

The southern recess opens directly into the main street and is flooded with light. Its floor is covered with large fragments of rock that have fallen from the cliff above. The spaces between these bowlders were filled with débris and the bowlders themselves were covered with the same accumulations the removal of which was no small task.

Minor Antiquities

The rooms and refuse-heaps of Spruce-tree House had been pretty thoroughly ransacked for specimens by those who preceded the author, so that few minor antiquities were expected to come to light in the excavation and repair work. Notwithstanding this, however, a fair collection, **contai**ning some unique specimens and many representative objects, was made, and is now in the National Museum where it will be preserved and be accessible to all students. Considering the fact that most of the specimens previously abstracted from this ruin have been scattered in all directions and are now in many hands, it is doubtful whether a collection of any considerable size from Spruce-tree House exists in any other public museum. In order to render this account more comprehensive, references are made in the following pages to objects from Spruce-tree House elsewhere described, now in other collections. These references, quoted from Nordenskiöld, the only writer on this subject, are as follows:

Plate XVIII: 2. a and b. Strongly flattened cranium of a child. Found in a room in Sprucetree House.

Plate XXXIV: 4. Stone axe of porphyrite. Sprucetree House.

Plate XXXV: 2. Rough-hewn stone axe of quartzite. Sprucetree House.

Plate XXXIX: 6. Implement of black slate. Form peculiar (see the text). Found in Sprucetree House.

[In the text the last-mentioned specimen is again referred to, as follows:]

I have still to mention a number of stone implements the use of which is unknown to me, first some large (15-30 cm.), flat, and rather thick stones of irregular shape and much worn at the edges (Pl. XXXIX: 4, 5), second a singular object consisting of a thin slab of black slate, and presenting the appearance shown in Pl. XXXIX: 6. My collection contains only one such implement, but among the objects in Wetherill's possession I saw several. They are all of exactly the same shape and of almost the same size. I cannot say in what manner this slab of slate was employed. Perhaps it is a last for the plaiting of sandals or the cutting of moccasins. In size it corresponds pretty nearly to the foot of an adult.

Plate XL: 5. Several *ulnæ* and *radii* of birds (turkeys) tied on a buckskin string and probably used as an amulet. Found in Sprucetree House.

Plate XLIII: 6. Bundle of 19 sticks of hard wood, probably employed in some kind of knitting or crochet work. The pins are pointed at one end, blunt at the other, and black with wear. They are held together by a narrow band of yucca. Found in Sprucetree House.

Plate XLIV: 2. Similar to the preceding basket, but smaller. Found in Sprucetree House....

[The "preceding basket" is thus described in explanation of the figure (Pl. XLIV: 1):] Basket of woven yucca in two different colors, a neat pattern being thus attained. The strips of yucca running in a vertical direction are of the natural yellowish brown, the others (in horizontal direction) darker....

Plate XLV: 1(95) and 2(663): Small baskets of yucca, of plain colour and of handsomely plaited pattern. Found: 1 in ruin 9, 2 in Sprucetree House.

Plate XLVIII: 4(674). Mat of plaited reeds, originally 1.2 × 1.2 m., but damaged in transportation. Found in Sprucetree House.

It appears from the foregoing that the following specimens have been described and figured by Nordenskiöld, from Spruce-tree House: (1) A child's skull; (2) 2 stone axes; (3) a slab of black slate; (4) several bird bones used for amulet; (5) bundle of sticks; (6) 2 small baskets; (7) a plaited mat.

In addition to the specimens above referred to, the majority of which are duplicated in the author's collection, no objects from Spruce-tree House are known to have been described or figured elsewhere, so that there are embraced in the present account practically all printed references to known material from this ruin. But there is no doubt that other specimens as yet unmentioned in print still exist in public collections in Colorado, and later these also may be described and figured. From the nature of the author's excavations and method of collecting, little hope remains that additional specimens may be obtained from rooms in Spruce-tree House, but the northern refuse-heap situated at the back of the cavern may yet yield a few good objects. This still awaits complete scientific excavation.

The author's collection from Spruce-tree House, the choice specimens of which are now in the National Museum, numbers several hundred objects. All the duplicates and heavy specimens, about equal in number to the lighter ones, were left at the ruin where they are available for future study. These are mostly stone mauls, metates and large grinding implements, and broken bowls and vases. The absence from Spruce-tree House of certain characteristic objects widely distributed among Southwestern ruins is regarded as worthy of comment. It will be noticed in looking over the author's collection that there are no specimens of marine shells, or of turquoise ornaments or obsidian flakes, from the excavations made at

Spruce-tree House. This fact is significant, meaning either that the former inhabitants of this village were ignorant of these objects or that the excavators failed to find what may have existed. The author accepts the former explanation, that these objects were not in use by the inhabitants of Spruce-tree House, their ignorance of them having been due mainly to their restricted commercial dealings with their neighbors.

Obsidian, one of the rarest stones in the cliff-dwellings of the Mesa Verde, as a rule is characteristic of very old ruins and occurs in those having kivas of the round type, to the south and west of that place.

It is said that turquoise has been found in the Mesa Verde ruins. The author has seen a beautiful bird mosaic with inlaid turquoise from one of the ruins near Cortez in Montezuma valley. This specimen is made of hematite with turquoise eyes and neckband of the same material; the feathers are represented by stripes of inlaid turquoise. Also inlaid in turquoise in the back is an hourglass figure, recalling designs drawn in outline on ancient pottery.

The absence of bracelets, armlets, and finger rings of sea shells, objects so numerous in the ruins along the Little Colorado and the Gila, may be explained by lack of trade, due to culture isolation. **The pe**ople of Mesa Verde appear not to have come in contact with tribes who traded these shells, consequently they never obtained them. The absence of culture connection in this direction tells in favor of the theory that the ancestors of the Mesa Verde people did not come from the southwest or the west, where shells are so abundant. Although not proving much either way by itself, this theory, when taken with other facts which admit of the same interpretation, is significant. The inhabitants of Spruce-tree House (the same is true of the other Mesa Verde people) had an extremely narrow mental horizon. They obtained little in trade from their neighbors and were quite unconscious of the extent of the culture of which they were representatives.

POTTERY

The women of Spruce-tree House were expert potters and decorated their wares in a simple but artistic manner. Until we have more material it would be gratuitous to assume that the ceramic art objects of all the Mesa Verde ruins are identical in texture, colors, and symbolism, and the only way to determine how great are the variations, if any, would be to make an accurate comparative study of pottery from different localities. Thus far the quantity of material available does not justify comparison even of the ruins of this mesa, but there is a good beginning of a collection from Spruce-tree House. The custom of placing in graves offerings of food for the dead has preserved several good bowls, and although whole pieces are rare fragments are found in abundance. Eighteen earthenware vessels, including those repaired and restored from fragments, rewarded the author's excavations at Spruce-tree

House. Some of these vessels bear a rare and beautiful symbolism which is quite different from that known from Arizona. The few plates (16-20) here given to illustrate these symbols are offered more as a basis for future study and comparisons than as an exhaustive representation of ceramics from one ruin.

The number and variety of pieces of pottery figured from the Mesa Verde cliff-dwellings have not been great. An examination of Nordenskiöld's memoir reveals the fact that he represents about 50 specimens of pottery; several of these were obtained by purchase, and others came from Chelly canyon, the pottery of which is strikingly like that of Mesa Verde. The majority of specimens obtained by Nordenskiöld's excavations were from Step House, not a single ceramic object from Spruce-tree House being figured. So far as the author can ascertain, the ceramic specimens here considered are the first representatives of this art from Spruce-tree House that have been described or figured, but there may be many other specimens from this locality awaiting description and it is to be hoped that some day these may be made known to the scientific world.

FORMS

Every form of pottery represented by Nordenskiöld, with the exception of that which he styles a "lamp-shaped" vessel and of certain platter forms with indentations, occurs in the collection here considered.

FIG. 1. Lid of jar.

Nordenskiöld figures a jar provided with a lid, both sides of which are shown.[22] It would seem that this lid (fig. 1),[23] unlike those provided with knobs, found by the author, had two holes near the center. The decoration on the top of the lid of one of the author's specimens resembles that figured by Nordenskiöld, but other specimens differ from his as shown in figure 1.

The specimens having raised lips and lids are perforated in the edges of the openings, with one or more holes for strings or handles. As bowls of this form are found in sacred rooms they would seem to have been connected with worship. The author believes that they served the same purposes as the netted gourds of the Hopi. Most of the ceramic objects in Spruce-tree House were in fragments when found.[24] Some of these objects have been repaired and it is remarkable that so much good material for the study of the symbolism has been obtained in this way.

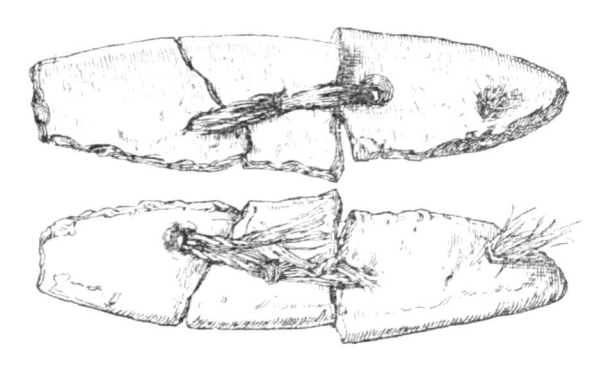

FIG. 2. Repaired pottery.

Black-and-white ware is the most common and the characteristic painted pottery, but fragmentary specimens of a reddish ware occur. One peculiarity in the lips of food bowls from Spruce-tree House (pls. 16-18) is that their rims are flat, instead of rounded as in more western prehistoric ruins, like Sikyatki. Food bowls are rarely concave at the base.

No fragments of glazed pottery were found, although the surfaces of some species were very smooth and glossy from constant rubbing with smoothing stones. Several pieces of pottery were unequally fired, so that a vitreous mass, or blotch, was evident on one side. Smooth vessels and those made of coiled ware, which were covered with soot from fires, were evidently used in cooking.

Several specimens showed evidences of having been broken and **afterw**ards mended by the owners (fig. 2); holes were drilled near the line of fracture and the two parts tied together; even the yucca strings still remain in the holes, showing where fragments were united. In figure 3 there is represented a fragment of a handle of an amphora on which is tied a tightly-woven cord.

FIG. 3. Handle with attached cord.

Not a very great variety of pottery forms was brought to light in the operations at Spruce-tree House. Those that were found are essentially the types common throughout the Southwest, and may be classified as follows: (1) Large jars, or ollas; (2) flat food bowls; (3) cups and mugs; (4) ladles or dippers (fig. 4); (5) canteens; (6) globular bowls. An exceptional form is a globular bowl with a raised lip like a sugar bowl (pl. 19, *f*). This form is never seen in other prehistoric ruins.

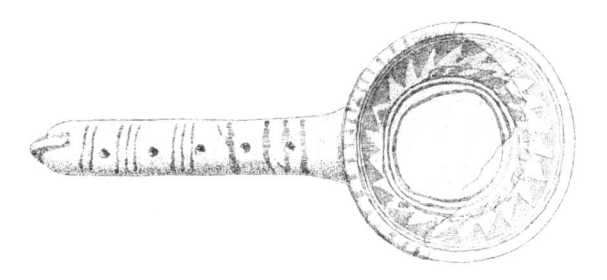

FIG. 4. Ladle.

STRUCTURE

Classified by structure, the pottery found in the Spruce-tree House ruin falls into two groups, coiled ware and smooth ware, the latter either with or without decoration. The white ware has black decorations.

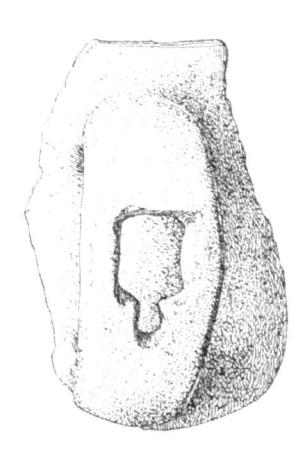

FIG. 5. Handle of mug.

The bases of the mugs (pl. 19) from Spruce-tree House, like those from other Mesa Verde ruins, have a greater diameter than the lips. These mugs are tall and their handles are of generous size. One of the mugs found in this ruin has a **T**-shaped hole in its handle (fig. 5), recalling in this particular a mug collected in 1895 by the author at Awatobi, a Hopi ruin.

The most beautiful specimen of canteen found at Spruce-tree House is here shown in plate 20.

The coiled ware of Spruce-tree House, as of all the Mesa Verde ruins, is somewhat finer than the coiled ware of Sikyatki. Although **no complete** specimen was found, many fragments were collected, some of which are of great size. This kind of ware was apparently the most abundant and also the most fragile. As a rule these vessels show marks of fire, soot, or smoke on the outside, and were evidently used as cooking vessels. On account of their fragile character they could not have been used for carrying water, for, with one or two exceptions, they would not be equal to the strain. In decoration of coiled ware the women of Spruce-tree House resorted to an ingenious modification of the coils, making triangular figures, spirals, or crosses in relief, which were usually affixed to the necks of the vessels.

The symbolism on the pottery of Spruce-tree House is essentially that of a cliff-dwelling culture, being simple in general characters. Although it has many affinities with the archaic symbols of the Pueblos, it has not the same complexity. The reason for this can be readily traced to that same environmental influence which caused the communities to seek the cliffs for protection. The very isolation of the Mesa Verde cliff-dwellings prevented the influx of new ideas and consequently the adoption of new symbols to represent them. Secure in their cliffs, the inhabitants were not subject to the invasion of strange clans nor could new customs be introduced, so that conservatism ruled their art as well as their life in general. Only simple symbols were present because there was no outside stimulus or competition to make them complex.

On classification of Spruce-tree House pottery according to technique, irrespective of its form, two divisions appear: (1) Coiled ware showing the coils externally, and (2) smooth ware with or without decorations. Structurally both divisions are the same, although their outward appearance is different.

The smooth ware may be decorated with incised lines or pits, but is painted often in one color. All the decorated vessels obtained by the author at Spruce-tree House belong to what is called black-and-white ware, by which is meant pottery having a thin white slip covering the whole surface upon which black pictures are painted. Occasionally fragments of a reddish brown cup were found, while red ware bearing white decorative figures was recovered from the Mesa Verde; but none of these are ascribed to Spruce-tree House or were collected by the author. The general geographical distribution of this black-and-white ware, not taking into account sporadic examples, is about the same as that of the circular kivas, but it is also found where circular kivas are unknown, as in the upper part of the valley of the Little Colorado.

The black-and-white ware of modern pueblos, as Zuñi and Hano, the latter the Tewan pueblo among the Hopi, is of late introduction from the Rio Grande; prehistoric Zuñi ware is unlike that of modern **Zuñi,** being practically identical in character with that of the other ancient pueblos of the Little Colorado and its tributaries.

Decoration

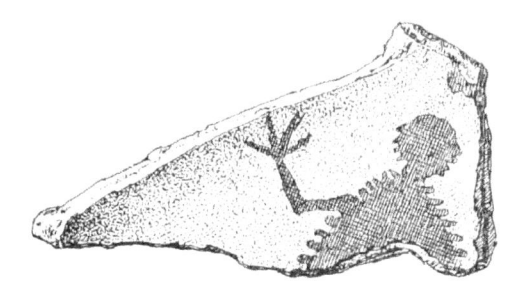

FIG. 6. Fragment of pottery.

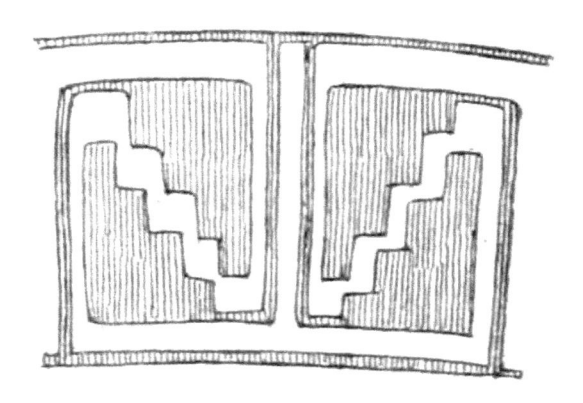

FIG. 7. Zigzag ornament.

As a rule, the decoration on pottery from Spruce-tree House is simple, being composed mainly of geometrical patterns. Life forms are rare, when present consisting chiefly of birds or rude figures of mammals painted on the outside of food bowls (fig. 6). The geometrical figures are principally rectilinear, there being a great paucity of spirals and curved lines. The tendency to arrange rows of dots along straight lines is marked in Mesa Verde pottery and occurs also in dados of house walls. There are many examples of stepped or terraced figures which are so arranged in pairs that the spaces between the terraces form zigzag bands, as shown in figure 7. A band extending from the upper left hand, to the lower right hand, angle of the rectangle that incloses the two terraced figures, may be designated a sinistral, and when at right angles a dextral, terraced figure (fig. 8). Specimens from Spruce-tree House show considerable modification in these two types.

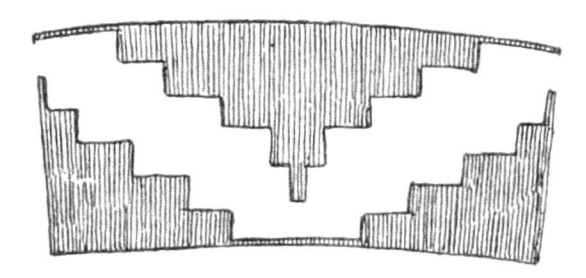

FIG. 8. Sinistral and dextral stepped figures.

With exception of the terrace the triangle (fig. 9) is possibly the most common geometrical decoration on Spruce-tree House pottery. Most of the triangles may be bases of terraced figures, for by cutting notches on the longer sides of these triangles, sinistral or dextral stepped figures (as the case may be) result.

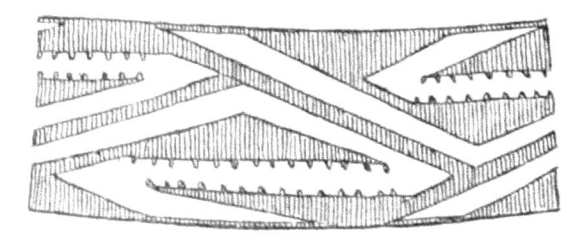

FIG. 9. Triangle ornament.

The triangles may be placed in a row, united in hourglass forms, or distributed in other ways. These triangles may be equilateral or one of the angles may be very acute. Although the possibilities of triangle combinations are almost innumerable the different forms can be readily recognized. The dot is a common form of decoration, and parallel lines also are much used. Many bowls are decorated with hachure, and with line ornaments mostly rectilinear.

The volute plays a part, although not a conspicuous one, in Spruce-tree House pottery decoration. Simple volutes are of two kinds, **one in** which the figure-coils follow the direction of the hands of the clock (dextral); the other, in which they take an opposite direction (sinistral). The outer end of the volute may terminate in a triangle or other figure, which may be notched, serrated, or otherwise modified. A compound sinistral volute is one which is sinistral until it reaches the center, when it turns into a dextral volute extending to the periphery. The compound dextral volute is exactly the reverse of the last-mentioned, starting as dextral and ending as sinistral. If, as frequently happens, there is a break in the lines at the middle, the figure may be called a broken compound volute. Two volutes having different axes are known as a composite volute, sinistral or dextral as the case may be.

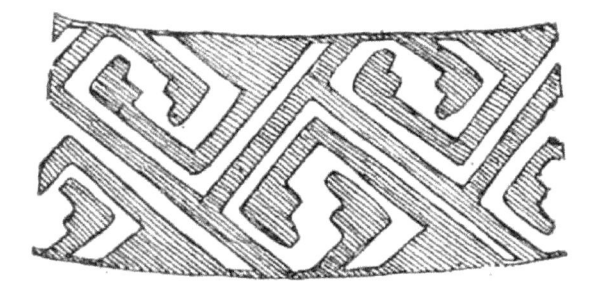

FIG. 10. Meander.

The meander (fig. 10) is also important in Spruce-tree House or Mesa Verde pottery decoration. The form of meander homologous to the volute may be classified in the same terms as the volute, into (1) simple sinistral meander; (2) simple dextral meander; (3) compound sinistral meander; (4) compound dextral meander; and (5) composite meander. These meanders, like the volutes, may be accompanied by parallel lines or by rows of dots enlarged, serrated, notched, or otherwise modified.

In some beautiful specimens a form of hachure, or combination of many parallel lines with spirals and meanders, is introduced in a very effective way. This kind of decoration is very rare on old Hopi (Sikyatki) pottery, but is common on late Zuñi and Hano ceramics, both of which are probably derived from the Rio Grande region.

Lines, straight or zigzag, constitute important elements in Spruce-tree House pottery decoration. These may be either parallel, or crossed so as to form reticulated areas.

Along these lines rows of dots or of triangular enlargements may be introduced. The latter may be simply serrations, dentations, or triangles of considerable size, sometimes bent over, resembling pointed bands.

Curved figures are rarely used, but such as are found are characteristic. Concentric rings, with or without central dots, are not uncommon.

Rectangles apparently follow the same general rules as circles, and are also sometimes simple, with or without central dots.

The triangle is much more common as a decorative motive than the circle or the rectangle, variety being brought about by the difference in length of the sides. The hourglass formed by two triangles with one angle of each united is common. The quail's-head design, or triangle **having** two parallel marks on an extension at one angle, is not as common as on Little Colorado pottery and that from the Gila valley.

As in all ceramics from the San Juan area, the stepped figures are most abundant. There are two types of stepped figures, the sinistral and the dextral, according as the steps pass from left to right or vice versa. The color of the two stepped figures may be black, or one or both may have secondary ornamentation in forms of hachure or network. One may be solid black, the other filled in with lines.

In addition to the above-mentioned geometrical figures, the S-shaped design is common; when doubled, this forms the cross called swastika. The S figure is of course generally curved but may be angular, in which case the cross is more evident. One bowl has the S figure on the outside. All of the above-mentioned designs admit of variations and two or more are often combined in Spruce-tree House pottery, which is practically the same in type as that of the whole Mesa Verde region.

CERAMIC AREAS

While it is yet too early in our study of prehistoric pueblo culture to make or define subcultural areas, it is possible to recognize provisionally certain areas having features in common, which differ from other areas.[25] It has already been shown that the form of the subterranean ceremonial room can be used as a basis of classification. If pottery symbols are taken as the basis, it will be found that there are at least two great subsections in the pueblo country coinciding with the two divisions recognized as the result of study of the form of sacred rooms—the northeastern and the southwestern region or, for brevity, the northern and the southern area. In the former region lie, besides the Mesa Verde and the San Juan valley, Chaco and Chelly canyons; in the latter, the ruins of "great houses" along the Gila and Salt rivers.

From these two centers radiated in ancient times two types of pottery symbols expressive of two distinct cultures, each ceremonially distinct and, architecturally speaking, characteristic. The line of junction of the influences of these two subcultural areas practically follows the Little Colorado river, the valley of which is the site of a third ceramic subculture area; this is mixed, being related on one side to the northern, on the other to the southern, region. The course of this river and its tributaries has determined a trail of migration, which in turn has spread this intermingled ceramic art far and wide. The geographical features of the Little Colorado basin have prevented the evolution of characteristic ceramic culture in any part of the region.

Using color and symbolism of pottery as a basis of classification, the author has provisionally divided the sedentary people of the Southwest into the following divisions, or has recognized the following ceramic areas: (1) Hopi area, including the wonderful ware of Sikyatki, Awatobi, and the ruins on Antelope mesa, at old Mishongnovi, Shumopavi and neighboring ruins; (2) Casa Grande area; (3) San Juan area, including Mesa Verde, Chaco canyon, Chelly canyon as far west as St. George, Utah, and Navaho mountain, Arizona; (4) Little Colorado area, including Zuñi. The pottery of Casas Grandes in Chihuahua is allied in colors but not in symbols to old Hopi ware. So little is known of the old Piros ceramics and of the pottery from all ruins east of the Rio Grande, that they are not yet classified. The ceramics from the region west of the Rio Grande are related to the San Juan and Chaco areas.

The Spruce-tree House pottery belongs to the San Juan area, having some resemblance and relationship to that from the lower course of the Little

Colorado. It is markedly different from the pottery of the Hopi area and has only the most distant resemblance to that from Casas Grandes.[26]

HOPI AREA

The Hopi area is well distinguished by specialized symbols which are not duplicated elsewhere in the pueblo area. Among these may be mentioned the symbol for the feather, and a band representing the sky with design of a mythic bird attached. As almost all pueblo symbols, ancient and modern, are represented on old Hopi ware, and in addition other designs peculiar to it, the logical conclusion is that these Hopi symbols are specialized in origin.

The evolution of a ceramic area in the neighborhood of the modern Hopi mesas is due to special causes, and points to a long residence in that locality. It would seem from traditions that the earliest Hopi people came from the east, and that the development of a purely Hopi ceramic culture in the region now occupied by this people took place before any great change due to southern immigration had occurred. The entrance of Patki and other clans from the south strongly affected the old Hopi culture, which was purest in Sikyatki, but even there it remained distinctive. The advent of the eastern clans in large numbers after the great rebellion in 1680, especially of the Tanoan families about 1710, radically changed the symbolism, making modern Hopi ware completely eastern in this respect. The old symbolism, the germ of which was eastern, as shown by the characters employed, almost completely vanished, being replaced by an introduced symbolism.

In order scientifically to appreciate the bearing on the migration of clans, of symbolism on pottery, we must bear in mind that a radical difference in such symbolism as has taken place at the Hopi villages may have occurred elsewhere as well, although there is no evidence of a change of this kind having occurred at Spruce-tree House.

The author includes under Hopi ware that found at the Hopi ruins Sikyatki, Shumopavi, and Awatobi, the collection from the first-named being typical. Some confusion has been introduced by others into the study of old Hopi ware by including in it, under the name "Tusayan pottery," the white-and-black ware of the Chelly canyon.[27] There is a close resemblance between the pottery of Chelly canyon and that of Mesa Verde, but only the most distant relationship between true Hopi ware and that of Chelly canyon. The latter belong in fact to two distinct areas, and differ in color, symbolism, and general characters. In so far as the Hopi ware shares its symbolism with the other geographical areas of the eastern region, to the same extent there is kinship in culture. In more distant ruins the pottery contains a greater admixture of symbols foreign to Mesa Verde. These differences are due no doubt to incorporation of other clans.

The subceramic area in which the Mesa Verde ruins lie embraces the valleys of the San Juan and its tributaries, Chelly canyon, Chaco canyon, and probably the ruins along the Rio Grande, on both sides of the river. Whether the Chaco or the Mesa Verde region is the geographical center of this subarea, or not, can not be determined, but the indications are that the Mesa Verde is on its northern border. Along the southwestern and western borders the culture of this area mingles with that of the subcultural area adjoining on the south, the resultant symbolism being consequently more complex. The ceramic ware of ruins of the Mesa Verde is little affected by outside and diverse influences, while, on the contrary, similar ware found along the western and southern borders of the subcultural area has been much modified by the influence of the neighboring region.

LITTLE COLORADO AREA

Although the decoration on pottery from Spruce-tree House embraces some symbols in common with that of the ruins along the Little Colorado, including prehistoric Zuñi, there is evidence of a mingling of the two ceramic types which is believed to have originated in the Gila basin. The resemblance in the pottery of these regions is greater near the sources of the Little Colorado, differences increasing as one descends the river. At Homolobi (near Winslow) and Chevlon, **where** the pottery is half northern and half southern in type, these differences have almost disappeared.

This is what might be expected theoretically, and is in accordance with legends of the Hopi, for the Little Colorado ruins are more modern than the round-kiva culture of Chaco canyon and Mesa Verde, and than the square-ceremonial-house culture of the Gila. The indications are that symbolism of the Little Colorado ruins is a composite, representative in about equal proportions of the two subcultures of the Southwest.[28]

As confirmatory of this suggested dual origin we find that the symbolism of pottery from ruins near the source of the Little Colorado is identical with that of the Salt, the Verde, and the Tonto basins, from which their inhabitants originally came in larger numbers than from the Rio Grande. In the ruins of the upper Salt and Gila the pottery is more like that of the neighboring sources of the Little Colorado because of interchanges. On the other hand, the ancient Hopi, being more isolated than other Pueblos, especially those on the Little Colorado, developed a ceramic art peculiar to themselves. Their pottery is different from that of the Little Colorado, the upper Gila and its tributary, the Salt, and the San Juan including the Mesa Verde.

The Zuñi valley, lying practically in the pathway of culture migration or about midway between the northern and southern subceramic areas, had no distinctive ancient pottery. Its ancient pottery is not greatly unlike that of

Homolobi near Winslow but has been influenced about equally by the northern and the southern type. Whatever originality in culture symbols developed in the Zuñi valley was immediately merged with others and spread over a large area.[29]

MESA VERDE AREA

While there are several subdivisions in the eastern subcultural area, that in which the Mesa Verde ruins are situated is distinctive. The area embraces the ruins in the Montezuma valley and those of Chelly canyon, and the San Juan ruins as far as Navaho mountain, including also the Chaco and the Canyon Largo ruins. Probably the pottery of some of the ruins east of the Rio Grande will be found to belong to the same type. That of the Hopi ceramic area, the so-called "Tusayan," exclusive of Chelly canyon, is distinct from all others. The pottery of the Gila subculture area is likewise distinctive but its influence made its way up the Verde and the Tonto and was potent across the mountains, in the Little Colorado basin. **Its in**fluence is likewise strong in the White Mountain ruins and on the Tularosa, and around the sources of the Gila and Salt rivers.

An examination of the decoration of pottery from Spruce-tree House fails to reveal a single specimen with the well-known broken encircling line called "the line of life." As this feature is absent from pottery from all the Mesa Verde ruins it may be said provisionally that the ancient potters of this region were unfamiliar with it.

This apparently insignificant characteristic is present, however, in all the pottery directly influenced by the culture of the southwestern subceramic area. It occurs in pottery from the Gila and the Salt River ruins, in the Hopi area, and along the Little Colorado, including the Zuñi valley, and elsewhere. Until recorded from the northeastern subceramic area, "the line of life" may be considered a peculiarity of ceramics of the Gila subarea or of the pottery influenced by its culture.

Among the restored food bowls from Spruce-tree House, having characteristic symbols, may be mentioned that represented in plate 16, *d, d'*, which has on the interior surface a triangular design with curved appendages to each angle. The triangular arrangement of designs on the interior surface of food bowls is not uncommon in the Mesa Verde pottery.

Another food bowl has two unusual designs on the interior surface, as shown in plate 18, *c, c'*. The meaning of this rare symbolism is unknown.

In plates 16-19 are represented some of the most characteristic symbols on the restored pottery.

The outer surfaces of many food bowls are elaborately decorated with designs as shown, while the rims in most cases are dotted.

STONE IMPLEMENTS

Stone implements from Spruce-tree House include axes, mauls, stone hammers, and grinding stones, in addition to other objects of unknown uses. As a rule these stone implements are rudely made, although some of them are as fine as any known from the Southwest. It is but natural that these implements should have been manufactured from more compact and harder rock than that of which the walls of the buildings were constructed. Apparently these objects were not picked up in the neighborhood but brought to the site of the ruin from a great distance.

AXES

The author collected several stone axes (pl. 21 and fig. 11) from Spruce-tree House, some of which (*a-f*) are fine specimens. These **are all** of the same general type, sharpened at one end and blunt at the opposite end, with a groove midway for attachment of the handle. In no case is there a ridge bordering this groove which in one specimen (pl. 21, *g*) is partially duplicated.

One ax has a cutting edge at each end, while another (fig. 12) has the handle still attached, recalling the two specimens figured by Nordenskiöld.

FIG. 11. Stone axes.

Among the objects of stone taken from Spruce-tree House are several similar to those called by the Hopi *tcamahias* (pl. 21, *h*). These implements are as a rule long, with smooth surfaces; they are sharpened at one end and pointed at the opposite end. Generally they have no groove for the attachment of a handle; in one instance, however, **there** is an indentation on opposite

- 42 -

borders. The use of these objects is unknown; they may have been axes or planting implements.

Stone objects of precisely the same type are highly prized by the Hopi and play important parts in their ceremonials. A number of these objects are arranged about the sand picture of the Antelope altar in the Snake dance at Walpi.[30]

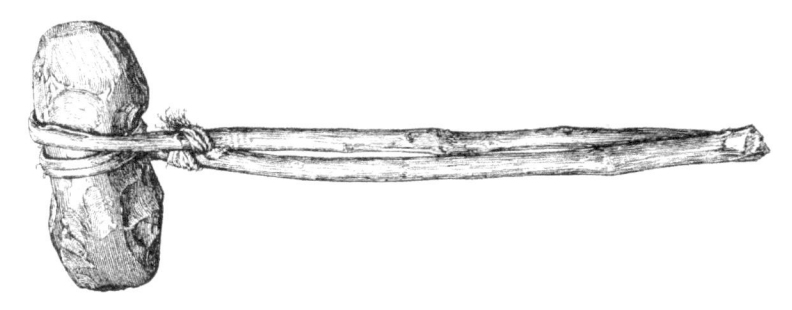

FIG. 12. Stone ax with handle.

Similar specimens are attached by the Hopi to their most sacred palladium, called the *tiponi*, or badge of office of the chief of a priesthood. The tiponi of the Antelope society has one of these projecting from its top. The meaning of this association may be even greater than at first would be suspected, for according to legends the Snake family, which is the guardian of the fetishes used in the snake ceremonies, originally lived at Tokonabi, near Navaho mountain, at the mouth of the San Juan river. The culture of the ancient inhabitants of the ruins at that place was not very different from that of the people of the Mesa Verde.

GRINDING STONES

Both pestles and hand stones used in grinding maize were excavated, the latter in considerable numbers. There were found also many stone slabs having rounded depressions, or pits, on opposite sides, evidently similar to those now used by the Hopi in grinding the paints for their ceremonials. In some places peckings or grooves in the surfaces of the rocks show where these grinding stones were used, and perhaps flattened to the desired plane. These grinding places are found in the plazas, on the sides of the cave back of the village, and elsewhere. A number of these grooves in a lower ledge of rock at the spring indicate that this was a favorite spot for shaping the hand grinders, possibly for grinding corn or other seeds.

The hand stones are of several types: (1) Polygonal, having corners somewhat worn, but flat on both sides, and having grooves on opposite edges to insure a firm hold for the hand; (2) convex on one **face a**nd flat on the opposite; (3) having two faces on each side, separated by a sharp ridge. The third type represents apparently the last stage in the life of a grinding stone the surfaces of which have been worn to this shape by constant use.

Several flat stones, each having a slight depression on one side, were found to be covered with pigments of various colors, which were ground on their surfaces by means of conical stones, as shown in figure 13. Two rectangular flat stones (pl. 21, *i, j*) with finely polished surfaces and rounded edges have a notch on the rim. Their use is unknown. Nordenskiöld refers to similar stones as "moccasin lasts," but there seems no valid reason thus to identify these objects except that they have the general form—although larger—of the sole of the foot. The Spruce-tree House aborigines wore sandals and had no need for lasts. Moreover, so far as known, the Pueblo Indians never made use of an object of this kind in fashioning their moccasins.

POUNDING STONES

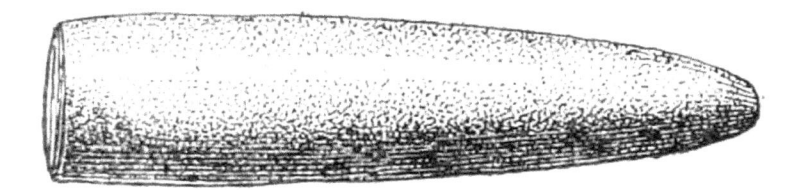

FIG. 13. Stone pigment-grinder.

In the course of the excavations a large number of stones having pits in the sides were exhumed, but these are so heavy that they were not sent to Washington. Several of these stones are cubical in form and have lateral pits, one on each of four faces. Some are thick, while others are thin and sharpened at the end like an ax. These stones are probably the mauls with which the masons dressed the rocks used in the construction of the buildings. With such mauls the surfaces of the floors of some ceremonial rooms were cut down several inches below the original level. Some of the pounding stones resemble in a measure the grinding stones, but in them pits replace grooves commonly found in the edge of the latter.

Corn was usually ground on flat stones called *metates* which were found in considerable numbers. These metates commonly show wear on one or both surfaces, and a few specimens have a ridge on each border resulting from the wearing down of the middle of the stone.

CYLINDER OF POLISHED HEMATITE

Among the objects from the ruins of Mesa Verde figured by Nordenskiöld is one designated a "cylinder of polished hematite, perhaps a fetish." Another stone cylinder closely resembling this was found by the present author at

Spruce-tree House. This object closely resembles a bead, but as the author has seen similar stones used on Hopi altars, especially on the altar to the cardinal points, he is inclined to accept the identification suggested by Nordenskiöld. On altars to the cardinal points small stones of different shapes and colors are arranged near ears of corn surrounding a medicine **bowl**. As black is the symbolic color of the underworld, a stone of this color is found on the black ear of corn representing the nadir. If this cylinder is a fetish it may have been somewhat similarly used.

BASKETRY

FIG. 14. Fragment of basket.

Not a single entire basket was found, although a few fragments of baskets made of woven rushes or osiers were obtained (fig. 14). It would appear, however, from a fine basket figured by Nordenskiöld, which he ascribes to Spruce-tree House and from other known specimens, figured and unfigured, that the Mesa Verde people were skillful basket makers. None of the fragments obtained by the author, and the same holds true regarding the basket figured by Nordenskiöld, are decorated.

WOODEN OBJECTS

Few objects made of wood were obtained at Spruce-tree House, but those which were found are well made and reveal the existence of interesting aboriginal customs. Wooden objects closely resembling some of these were used until a few years ago by the Hopi and other Pueblo tribes.

STICKS TIED TOGETHER

FIG. 15. Sticks tied together.

Among the wooden objects found are many perforated sticks tied together by strings. This specimen (fig. 15) is not complete, but enough remains to show that it is not unlike the covering in which the Hopi bride rolls her wedding blankets. From the place where the object was found, it appears that the dead were wrapped in coverings of this kind. Although the specimen is much damaged, it is not **diffic**ult to make out from the remaining fragment the mode of construction of the object.

SLABS

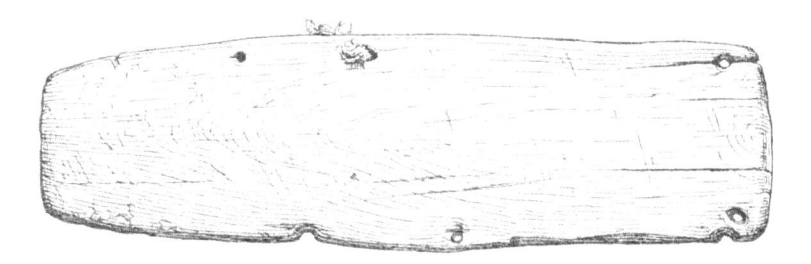

FIG. 16. Wooden slab.

Nordenskiöld figures a wooden object of rectangular shape, slightly concave on one side and more or less worn on the edges. Two similar wooden slabs (fig. 16) were found at Spruce-tree House. The objects occasioned much speculation, as their meaning is unknown. It has been suggested they are cradle-boards, a conjecture which, in view of the fact that similar specimens are sometimes found in child burials, is plausible. In this interpretation the holes which occur on the sides may have served for attachment of blankets or hoops. These boards, it may be said, are small even for the most diminutive Indian baby.

Another suggestion not without merit is that these boards are priest's badges and were once carried in the hands suspended by strings tied to the holes in their edges.

Still another theory identifies them as parts of head dresses called tablets, worn in what the Pueblos call a *tablita* dance.

The upright portions of some of the Hopi altars have similar wooden slabs painted with symbolic figures and tied together. Altars having slabs of the same description are used in ceremonials of certain Tewan clans living in New Mexico.

SPINDLES

FIG. 17. Spindle and whorl.

There were found at Spruce-tree House a complete spindle with stick and whorl (fig. 17), and a whorl without the spindle, both of which are practically identical in type with the spinning apparatus of the Hopi Indians. When in use this spindle was made to revolve by rubbing it on the thigh with one hand, while the other held the unspun cotton, the fiber being wound on one end of the spindle. This implement affords still another indication that the arts of the people of Spruce-tree House were similar to those still practised by the Pueblos.

PLANTING-STICKS

A few sticks which resemble those used by the Hopi as dibbles were collected at Spruce-tree House. These measure several feet in length; they are flat at one end, while the opposite end is pointed and rubbed down to a sharp edge. Some of these implements were slightly bent at one extremity.

MISCELLANEOUS OBJECTS

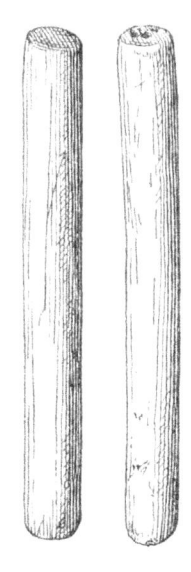

FIG. 18. Ceremonial sticks.

Among various wooden objects found at Spruce-tree House may be mentioned sticks resembling prayer offerings and others which may have been employed in ceremonials (fig. 18.)

A fragment of a primitive fire-stick (fig. 19) was obtained from the northern refuse-heap and near it were straight sticks that undoubtedly served as fire-drills. There were one or two needles (fig. 20), made of hard wood, suggesting weaving or some similar process. A fragment of an arrow was unearthed in the débris of the northern refuse-heap.

FIG. 19. Primitive fire-stick.

FIG. 20. Wooden needle.

FABRICS

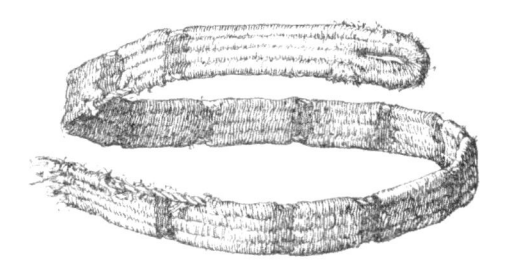

FIG. 21. Belt.

The yucca plant, which grows wild in the canyons and level places of the Mesa Verde, furnishes a tough fiber which the prehistoric people of Spruce-tree House used in the manufacture of various fabrics. Small packages of this fiber and cords made of the same material were found in the refuse-heap and in the houses; these were apparently obtained by heating and chewing the leaves, after which the fiber was drawn out into cords or braided into strings.

A braided cord was also found attached to the handles of jars, and this fiber was a favorite one in mending pottery. It was almost universally employed in weaving cloth netting and other fabrics, **where** it was combined with cotton fiber. Belts (fig. 21) or headbands (figs. 22, 23) show the best examples of this weaving. Native cotton fiber is not as common as yucca, being more difficult apparently to procure. There is some doubt regarding the cultivation of the cotton plant, and no cotton seeds were identified; the cloth woven from this fiber shows great skill in weaving.

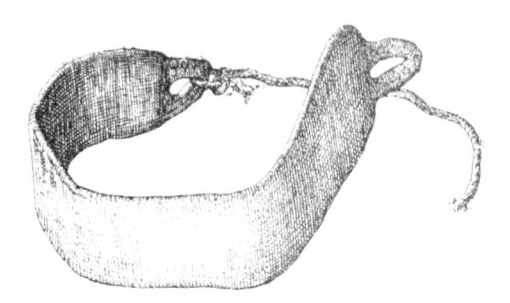

FIG. 22. Headband.

The bark of willows and alders was utilized for fabrics, but this furnished material for basketry rather than for cloth.

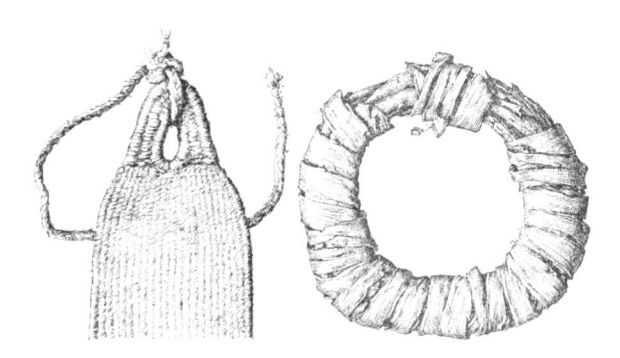

FIG. 23. End of headband. Fig. 24. Head ring.

One of the most beautiful specimens of woven cloth yet obtained in the Mesa Verde ruins was taken from room 11; this is apparently a headband for carrying bundles.

Among the objects obtained in the northern refuse-heap were rings made of the leaf and fiber of yucca and other plants, sometimes blackened as if by fire (fig. 24). These rings may have been used **for ca**rrying jars on the head, although some are too large and flat for that purpose. It has been suggested that the largest were used in some game, but this theory lacks confirmation.

Small fragments of matting were found, but no complete specimen came to light. These fragments resemble those referred to by Nordenskiöld as "objects used in carpeting the floors." It was customary among some of the sedentary Indians of the Southwest to sleep on rectangular mats, and in one building of compound B of Casa Grande impressions of these mats were found on the floor.

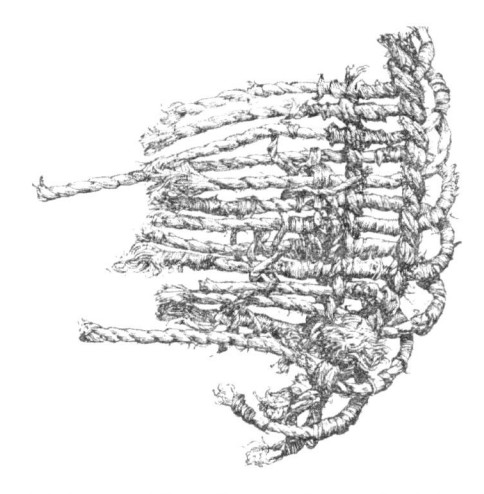

FIG. 25. Yucca-fiber cloth with attached feathers.

Fragments of cloth made of yucca fiber (fig. 25), in which feathers are woven, are abundant in the refuse-heaps of Spruce-tree House. There were found also many strings in which feathers were woven (fig. 26), but of these nothing but the midribs remain.

FIG. 26. Woven cord.

The object shown in figure 27 is made of agave fiber tied in a series of loops. Its use is unknown.

Several sandals were excavated at Spruce-tree House, the majority from the refuse-heap in the rear of the dwellings. One of these **specim**ens, figure 28, is in good condition; it is evidently a mortuary object, being found near a skeleton. The other specimen (fig. 29) is fragmentary, consisting of a sole of a sandal with attached toe cords.

FIG. 27. Agave fiber tied in loops.

FIG. 28. Woven moccasin.

FIG. 29. Fragment of sandal.

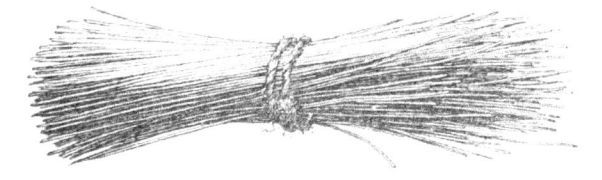

FIG. 30. Hair-brush.

Several specimens of slender yucca leaves bound in a bundle were found. One of these (fig. 30) served as a hair-brush, or was used in stirring food. One brush made of finer material was collected.

BONE IMPLEMENTS

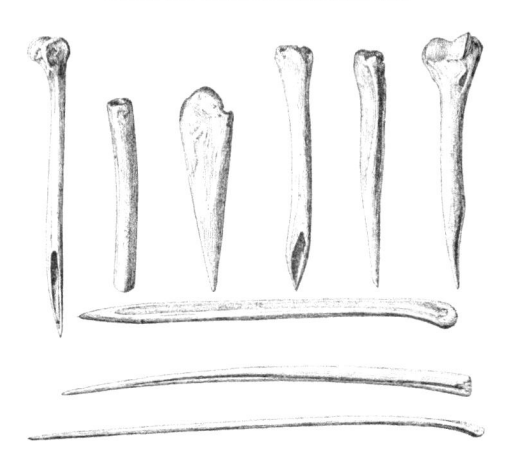

FIG. 31. Bone implements.

A large collection of beautiful bone implements (see fig. 31)—needles, awls, tubes, and dirks—rewarded the work at Spruce-tree House. Some of these show the effects of fire throughout their length, while others are smoked only at one end. When unearthed, one of these dirks was still in the original sheath of cedar bark (fig. 32).

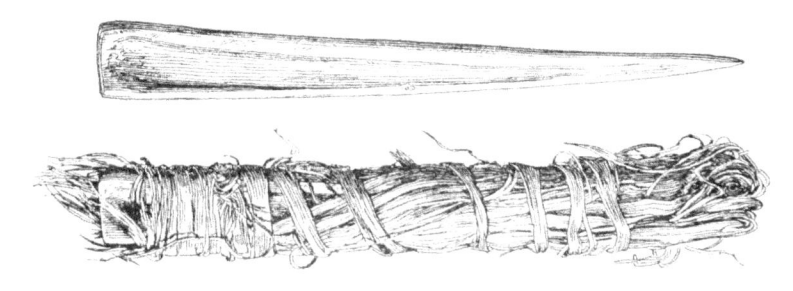

FIG. 32. Dirk and cedar-bark sheath.

Most of the needles, bodkins, and awls are made of bones of birds or small animals. These were apparently rubbed down and pointed on stone implements or on the sides of the cliff, where grooves are often found (fig. 33).

FIG. 33. Bone implement.

FIG. 34. Bone scraper.

Several fine bone scrapers (figs. 34, 35) were dug out of the débris covering the floors of the rooms. These are beveled to a sharp edge at one end, the trochanter of the bone serving as a handle.

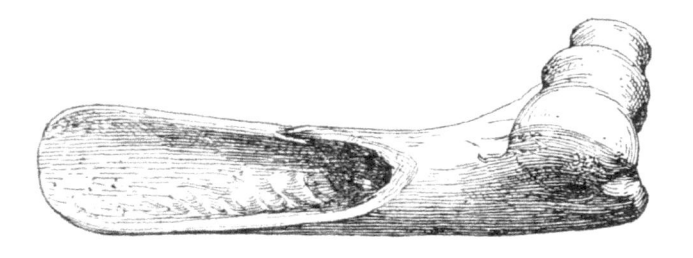

FIG. 35. Bone scraper.

FETISH

Only one fetish in the form of a human being was obtained at Spruce-tree House, this being found in the débris near the floor of kiva G. So far as the objects from Mesa Verde ruins have been figured or described, this is the first record of the finding of a fetish of human shape in any of these ruins. Moreover, such a fetish is a rarity in cliff-house ruins elsewhere in the Southwest, a fact which imparts to this specimen more than usual interest.

LIGNITE GORGET

In the author's account of his excavations in ruins in the Little Colorado valley there was figured a large fragment of a disk made of cannel coal or lignite. This disk is convex on one side and plain on the side opposite, the latter having an eyelet, or two holes for suspension. A lignite gorget, similar for the most part to the above-mentioned specimen, but differing therefrom in having the eyelet in **the co**nvex instead of in the flat side, was found at Spruce-tree House. Probably both objects were formerly used as ornaments, being suspended about the neck. No similar specimen has thus far been described from Mesa Verde ruins.

CORN, BEANS, AND SQUASH SEEDS

All indications point to maize, or Indian corn, as the chief food plant of the prehistoric people of this cliff-dwelling. This is evident not only from the presence in the ruins of metates and grinding stones, but also from the abundance of corn ears and other fragments discovered; corn husks and seed corn were especially plentiful in rooms and in the refuse-heaps. As in the case of the modern Pueblos, the corn appears to have been of several colors, while the size of the cobs indicates that the ears were small with but few rows of seeds. In addition to cobs, fragments of corn stalks, leaves, and even tassels were found in some of the rooms. Beans of the brown variety, specimens of which were numerous in one room, were the most esteemed. There were obtained also stalks and portions of gourds some of which are artificially perforated, as well as a gourd the rind of which is almost complete. Apparently these gourds were used for ceremonial rattles and for drinking vessels. The form suggests that of a Hopi netted gourd in which sacred water is brought from distant springs for use in the kivas, or ceremonial rooms.

HOOP-AND-POLE GAME

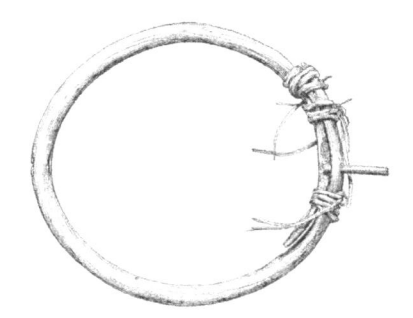

FIG. 36. Hoop used in hoop-and-pole game.

It appears from the discovery of a small wooden hoop in one of the rooms that the prehistoric people of Spruce-tree House were familiar with the hoop-and-pole game (fig. 36) so popular among several of our aboriginal tribes. But whether or not the individual **hoop o**btained was used in a secular game or a ceremony may be open to differences of opinion. The author is inclined to connect the specimen above referred to with basket dances, one of which is called by the Hopi the *Owakulti*.[31] In this dance the hoop is rolled on the ground and the players throw or attempt to throw darts through it.

LEATHER AND SKIN OBJECTS

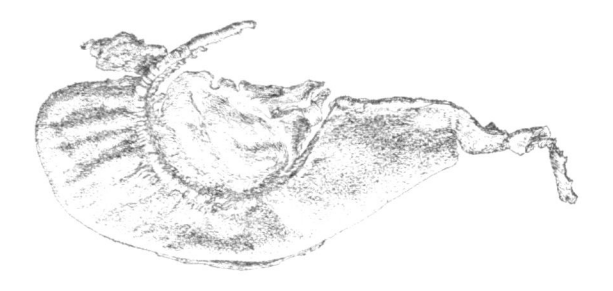

FIG. 37. Portion of leather moccasin.

Fragments of leather or dressed skin (fig. 37) were found in several of the rooms. These are apparently parts of moccasins or sandals, but may have been pouches or similar objects. A strip of rawhide by means of which an ax was lashed to its handle was picked up in the dump, where also was a fragment of what may have been a leather pouch with a thong of hide woven in one edge. If skins of animals were used for clothing, as they probably were, but slight evidence of the fact remains.

ABSENCE OF OBJECTS SHOWING EUROPEAN CULTURE

In the excavations which were necessary to clean out the rooms of Spruce-tree House no object of European make was discovered. There was no sign of any metal, even copper being unrepresented; no object discovered shows traces of cutting by knives or other implements made of metal. Evidently European culture exerted no influence on the aborigines of Spruce-tree House.

PICTOGRAPHS

Near Spruce-tree House, as elsewhere on the Mesa Verde, are found examples of those rock-etchings and other markings known as pictographs. Some of these represent human beings in various attitudes, and animals, as deer, mountain sheep, snakes, and other subjects not **yet de**termined. As seems to be true of the other rock-inscriptions just mentioned, some of those near Spruce-tree House are religious symbols, some are totems, while others are mere scribblings.

These pictographs are so rude that they give little idea of the artistic possibilities of their makers, while many are so worn that even the subjects intended to be depicted are doubtful.

The walls of some of the rooms in the Mesa Verde cliff-dwellings still show figures painted while the rooms were inhabited. Among these the favorite designs are of triangular form.

The walls of the secular rooms and kivas of Spruce-tree House were formerly covered with a thin wash of colored sand which was well adapted for paintings of symbolic or decorative character. The colors (yellow, red, and white), were evidently put on with the hands, impressions of which can be found in several places. In some cases, as with the upper part of the wall painted white and the lower part red, the contrast brings out the colors very effectively. The walls of some of the rooms are blackened with smoke.

Among the designs used are the triangular figures on the upper margin of the dados and pedestals of kivas. Figures similar in form, but reversed, are made by the Hopi, who call them butterfly and raincloud symbols.

Birds and quadrupeds.—Nordenskiöld (pp. 108-9) thus writes of one of the ancient paintings:

> The first of them, fig. 77, is executed in a room at Sprucetree House. Here too the lower part of the mural surface is dark red, and triangular points of the same colour project over the yellow plaster; above this lower part of the wall runs a row of red dots, exactly as in the estufa at Ruin 9. To the left two figures are painted, one of them evidently representing a bird, the other a quadruped with large horns, probably a mountain sheep.

[Elsewhere, as quoted on p. 5, Nordenskiöld identifies these figures as "two birds."] The painting shown in fig. 78 is similar in style to the two just described.

In this room the dado bears at intervals along its upper edge the triangular figures already noticed, and rows of dots which appear to be a symbolic decoration, occurring likewise on pottery, as an examination of the author's collection makes evident.

Square figures.—On the eastern wall of the same room in which occur the figures of a bird and a horned mammal there is a square figure on the white surface of the upper wall. This figure is black in outline; part of the surface bears an angular meander similar to decorations on some pieces of pottery. Similar designs, arranged in series according to Mindeleff's figures, form the decoration band of one of the kivas in Chelly canyon.

The significance of this figure is unknown but its widespread distribution, especially in that region of the Southwest characterized by circular kivas, adds considerable interest to its interpretation.

Terraced *figure.*—Covering almost the whole side of a wall north of kiva C and overlooking the plaza of which this room forms in part the northern wall, is a conspicuous figure painted white. If we regard the building of which this is a side as formerly two stories high, this painting would have been on the inside of a room, otherwise we have the exceptional feature of a painting on an outer wall. The purpose of this painting is not clear to the author, but similar figures, reversed, signify rain clouds. The figure recalls in form a representation of a **T**-shaped doorway and appears to be a unique one among Mesa Verde ruins.

CONCLUSIONS

From the preceding facts it is evident that the people who once inhabited Spruce-tree House were not highly developed in culture, although the buildings show an advanced order of architecture for aborigines of North America. Architecturally the cliff-dwellings excel pueblos of more recent construction.

The pottery Is not inferior to that of other parts of the Southwest, but has fewer symbols and is not as fine or varied in colors as that from Sikyatki or from Casas Grandes in Sonora. It is better than the pottery from the Casa Grande and other compounds of the Gila and about the same in texture and symbols as that from Chelly canyon and Chaco canyon.

The remaining minor antiquities, as cloth, basketry, wood, and bone, are of the same general character as those found elsewhere in the Southwest. Shell work is practically lacking; no objects made from marine shells have been found.

The picture of culture drawn from what we know of the life at Spruce-tree House is practically the same as that of a pueblo like Walpi at the time of its discovery by whites, and until about fifty years ago. The people were farmers, timid, industrious, and superstitious. The women were skillful potters and made fine baskets. The men made cloth of good quality and cultivated corn, beans, and melons.

In the long winters the kivas served as the lounging places for the men who were engaged in an almost constant round of ceremonies of dramatic character, which took the place of the pleasures of the chase. They never ventured far from home and rarely met strangers. They had all those unsocial characteristics which an isolated life fosters.

What language they spoke, and whether various Mesa Verde Houses had the same language, at present no one can tell. The culture was selfcentered and apparently well developed. It is not **known** whether it originated in the Mesa Verde canyons or was completely evolved when it reached there.

Although we know little about the culture of the prehistoric inhabitants of Mesa Verde, it does not follow that we can not find out more. There are many ruins awaiting exploration in this region and future work will reveal much which has been so long-hidden.

The pressure of outside tribes, or what may be called human environment, probably had much to do originally with the choice of caves for houses, and the magnificent caverns of the Mesa Verde naturally attracted men as favorable sites for their houses. The habit of huddling together in a limited space, necessitated by a life in the cliffs, possibly developed the composite form which still persists in the pueblo form of architecture.

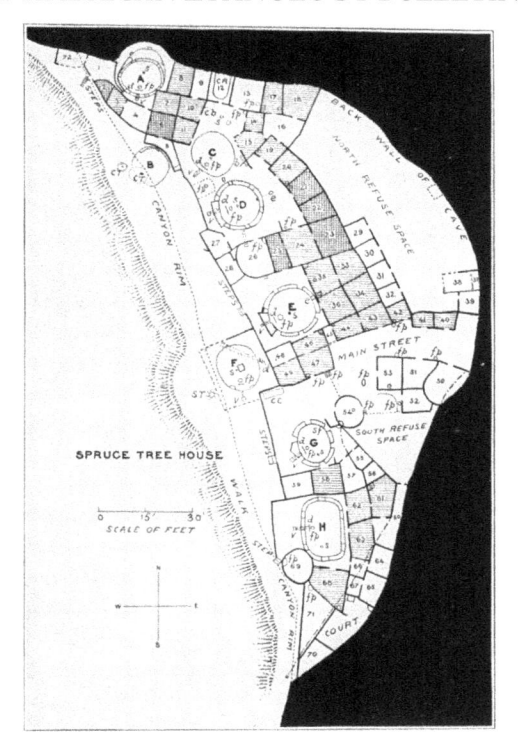

BUREAU OF AMERICAN ETHNOLOGY BULLETIN 41 PLATE 1

GROUND PLAN OF SPRUCE-TREE HOUSE

BUREAU OF AMERICAN ETHNOLOGY BULLETIN 41 PLATE 2

From the northwest

From the west. The ruin
THE RUIN, FROM THE NORTHWEST AND THE WEST

BUREAU OF AMERICAN ETHNOLOGY BULLETIN 41 PLATE 3

Before repairing

After repairing
PLAZA D

Before repairing

After repairing
THE RUIN, FROM THE SOUTH END

BUREAU OF AMERICAN ETHNOLOGY BULLETIN 41 PLATE 5

THE RUIN, FROM THE SOUTH

BUREAU OF AMERICAN ETHNOLOGY BULLETIN 41 PLATE 6

General view

Room 11, from the south
ROOMS 11-24

BUREAU OF AMERICAN ETHNOLOGY BULLETIN 41 PLATE 7

THE RUIN, FROM THE NORTH END

NORTH END OF THE RUIN, SHOWING MASONRY PILLAR

BUREAU OF AMERICAN ETHNOLOGY BULLETIN 41 PLATE 9

Roof of room 43

Main street
A ROOF AND A STREET

Front of rooms 62 and 63

Plaza E. from the south, before repair
THE RUIN FROM THE SOUTH END, SHOWING ROOMS AND PLAZA

Before repairing

After repairing
KIVA D

BUREAU OF AMERICAN ETHNOLOGY BULLETIN 41 PLATE 12

KIVA D, FROM THE NORTH

BUREAU OF AMERICAN ETHNOLOGY BULLETIN 41 PLATE 13

Kiva A, repaired

Kiva D, repaired
INTERIORS OF TWO KIVAS

BUREAU OF AMERICAN ETHNOLOGY BULLETIN 41 PLATE 14

From stump of spruce tree, looking east

Interior of kiva C. looking southwest
CENTRAL PART OF RUIN, AND KIVA

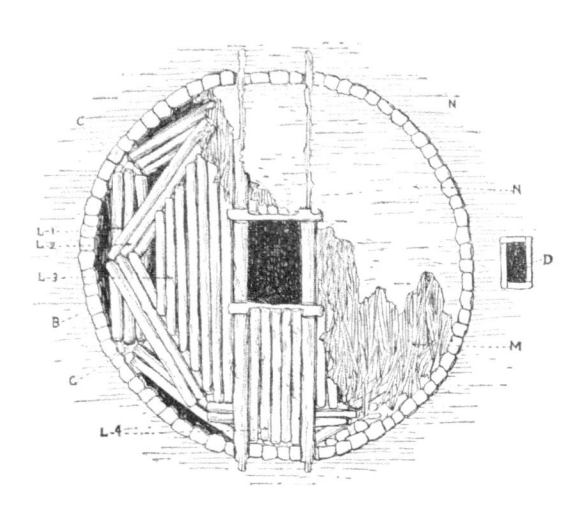

BUREAU OF AMERICAN ETHNOLOGY BULLETIN 41 PLATE 15

From above, showing roof

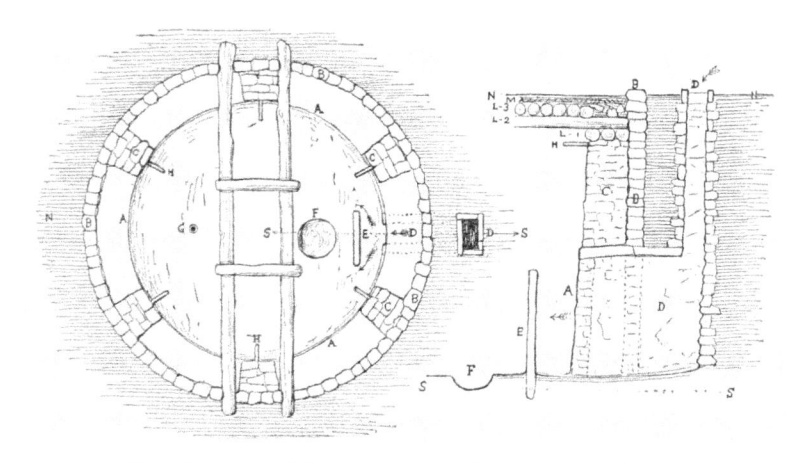

Roof removed Section of air-shaft, or ventilator
DIAGRAMS OF KIVA, SHOWING CONSTRUCTION

BUREAU OF AMERICAN ETHNOLOGY BULLETIN 41 PLATE 16

DECORATED FOOD-BOWLS
Diameters (in inches): a, a', 11¼; b, b', 11; c, c', 11½; d, d', 9⅛

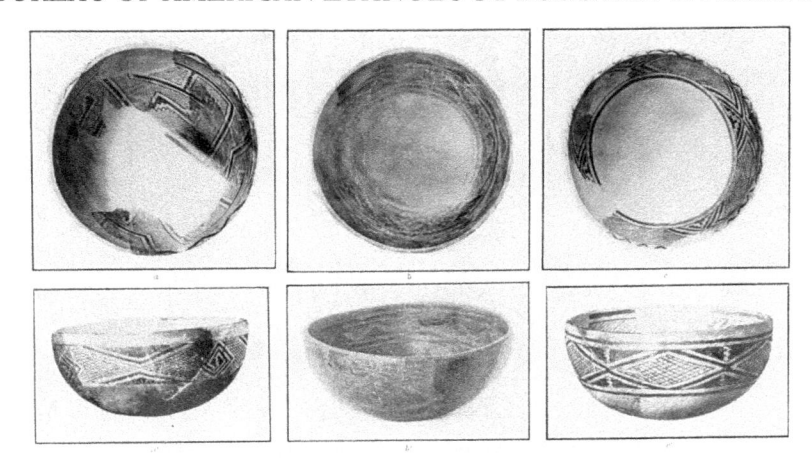

BUREAU OF AMERICAN ETHNOLOGY BULLETIN 41 PLATE 17

DECORATED FOOD-BOWLS
Diameters (in inches): a, a', 11; b, b', 13; c, c', 11¼

BUREAU OF AMERICAN ETHNOLOGY BULLETIN 41 PLATE 18

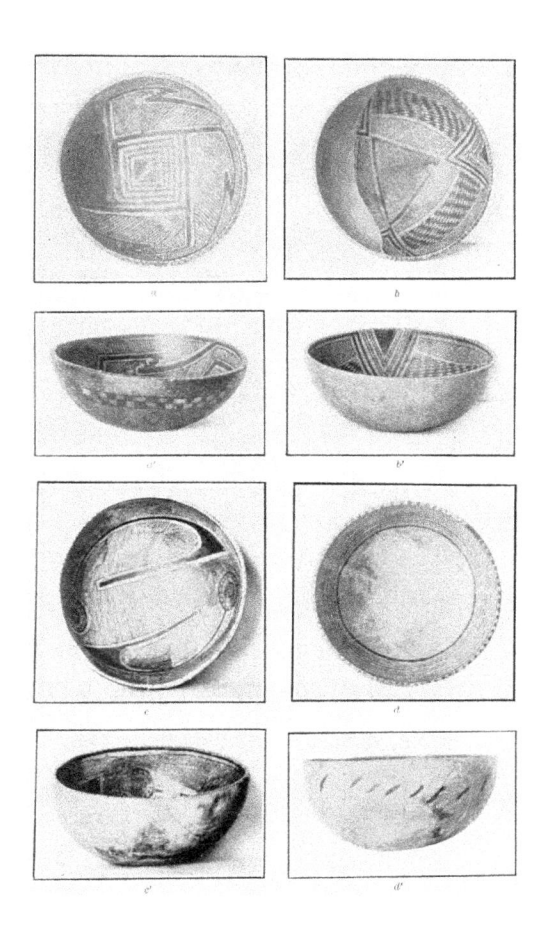

DECORATED FOOD-BOWLS
Diameters (in inches): *a, a'*, 9; *b, b'*, 12¼; *c, c'*, 11; *d, d'*, 11¾

BUREAU OF AMERICAN ETHNOLOGY BULLETIN 41 PLATE 19

DECORATED VASE AND MUGS
Heights (in inches): a, 3½; b, 3⅜; c, 3⅝; d, 4½; e, 3¾; f, 5

BUREAU OF AMERICAN ETHNOLOGY BULLETIN 41 PLATE 20

a. Small bowl (diam., 3¾ in.)

b. Two-handled globular canteen (height, 7¼ in.)
DECORATED BOWL AND CANTEEN

BUREAU OF AMERICAN ETHNOLOGY BULLETIN 41 PLATE 21

STONE IMPLEMENTS
a-g, axes; *h*, tcamahia; *i*, paint stone; *j*, paint stone (last?)
Lengths (in inches): *a*, 4¼; *b*, 4¾; *c*, 5; *d*, 5¼; *e*, 6¼; *f*, 6⅞; *g*, 5¾; *h*, 10½; *i*, 10½; *j*, 10¾

FOOTNOTES:

[1] The photographs from which plates 2-4, 6, 8-14 were made were taken by Mr. J. Nussbaum, photographer of the Archæological Institute of America.

[2] Ancient Ruins in Southwestern Colorado, in Rep. U. S. Geol. and Geogr. Survey of the Ter., 1874, p. 369.

[3] Report on the Ancient Ruins of Southwestern Colorado, examined during the summers of 1875 and 1876, ibid., 1876, p. 383.

[4] The Cliff Dwellers of the Mesa Verde, pp. 12, 13, Stockholm, 1893.

[5] Cliff-dwellings of the Mancos Cañons, in *Appalachia*, VI, no. 1, Boston, May, 1890; *The American Antiquarian*, XII, 193, 1890; The Land of the Cliff Dwellers, 1892.

[6] The Cliff-dwellings of the Cañons of the Mesa Verde, in *Bulletin of the American Geographical Society*, XXIII, no. 4, 584, 1891.

[7] Since this was written, a well-preserved mummy has been found by Wetherill in the open space (28) at the very back of the cave. This is a further example of the burial of the dead in the open space between the village and the cliff wall behind it (see p. 47).—[NORDENSKIÖLD.]

[8] On the author's plan of Spruce-tree House from a survey by Mr. S. G. Morley, the third story is indicated by crosshatching, the second by parallel lines, while the first has no markings. (Pl. 1.)

[9] See H. R. No. 3703, 58th Cong., 3d sess., 1905.—The Ruined Cliff Dwellings in Ruin and Navajo Canyons, in the Mesa Verde, Colorado, by Coert Dubois.

[10] See *American Anthropologist*, n. s., v. no. 2, 224-288, 1903.

[11] In Hopi dwellings the author has often seen a provisional *sipapû* used in household ceremonies.

[12] The proportion of kivas to dwellings in any village is not always the same in prehistoric pueblos, nor is there a fixed ratio in modern pueblos. It would appear that there is some relation between the number of kivas and the number of inhabitants, but what that relation is, numerically, has never been discovered.

[13] Nordenskiöld on the contrary seems to make the terraced rooms one of the points of resemblance between the cliff-dwellings and the great ruins of the Chaco. He writes:

"On comparison of the ruins in Chaco Cañon with the cliff-dwellings of Mancos, we find several points of resemblance. In both localities the villages are fortified against attack, in the tract of Mancos by their site in inaccessible precipices, in Chaco Cañon by a high outer wall in which no doorways were constructed to afford entrance to an enemy. Behind this outer wall the rooms descended in terraces towards the inner court. One side of this court was protected by a lower semicircular wall. In the details of the buildings we can find several features common to both. The roofs between the stories were constructed in the same way. The doorways were built of about the same dimensions. The rafters were often allowed to project beyond the outer wall as a foundation for a sort of balcony (Balcony House, the Pueblo Chettro Kettle). The estufa at Hungo Pavie with its six quadrangular pillars of stone is exactly similar to a Mesa Verde estufa (see p. 16). The pottery strewn in fragments everywhere in Chaco Cañon resembles that found on the Mesa Verde. We are thus not without grounds for assuming that it was the same people, at different stages of its development, that inhabited these two regions."—The Cliff Dwellers of the Mesa Verde, p. 127.

[14] Ibid., p. 67.

[15] *Bulletin 35 of the Bureau of American Ethnology*, Antiquities of the Upper Gila and Salt River Valleys in Arizona and New Mexico.

[16] In some cases the walls of the later rectangular rooms are built across and above them, as in compound B in the Casa Grande group of ruins.

[17] An examination of the best of previous maps of Spruce-tree House shows only a dotted line to indicate the location of this kiva.

[18] It has no doubt occurred to others, as to the author, that the number of Spruce-tree House kivas is a multiple of four, the number of horizontal cardinal points. Later it may be found that there is some connection between them and world-quarter clan ownership, or it may be that the agreement in numbers is purely a coincidence.

[19] The Cliff Dwellers of the Mesa Verde, p. 63.

[20] In clearing the kivas several fragments of human bones and skulls were found by the author. The horizontal passageways, called ventilators, of four of the kivas furnished a single broken skull each, which had not been buried with care.

[21] From the great amount of bird-lime and bones in these heaps it has been supposed that turkeys were domesticated and kept in these places.

[22] See The Cliff Dwellers of the Mesa Verde, pls. XXVIII, XXIX: 7.

[23] The text figures which appear in this paper were drawn from nature by Mrs. M. W. Gill, of Forest Glen, Md.

[24] The author is greatly indebted to Mr. A. V. Kidder for aid in sorting and labeling the fragments of pottery. Without his assistance in the field it would have been impossible to repair many of these specimens.

[25] The classification into cavate houses, cliff-dwellings, and pueblos is based on form.

[26] The above classification coincides in some respects with that obtained by using the forms of ceremonial rooms as the basis.

[27] Of 40 pieces of pottery called "Tusayan," figured in Professor Holmes' Pottery of the Pueblo Area (*Second Annual Report of the Bureau of Ethnology*), all but three or possibly four came from Chelly canyon and belong to the San Juan rather than to the Hopi ware. Black-and-white pottery is very rare in collections of old Hopi ware, but is most abundant in the cliff-houses of Chelly canyon and the Mesa Verde ruins.

[28] The pottery from ruins in the Little Colorado basin, from Wukoki at Black Falls to the Great Colorado, is more closely allied to that of the drainage of the San Juan and its tributaries.

[29] There is of course very little ancient Zuñi ware in museums, but such as we have justifies the conclusion stated above.

[30] Snake Ceremonials at Walpi, in *Journal of American Archæology and Ethnology*, IV, 1894.

[31] See figure of Owakulti altar in the author's account of the Owakulti. Mr. Stewart Culin thus comments on the "hoop-and-pole" game among Pueblos: "Similar ceremonies or games were practised by the cliff-dwellers, as is attested by a number of objects from Mancos canyon, Colorado, in the Free Museum of Science and Art of the University of Pennsylvania."—*Twenty-fourth Annual Report of the Bureau of American Ethnology*.